Also by Andy Cohen

Superficial:
More Adventures from the Andy Cohen Diaries

The Andy Cohen Diaries:
A Deep Look at a Shallow Year

Most Talkative:
Stories from the Front Lines of Pop Culture

GLITTER
EVERY DAY

GLITTER
EVERY DAY

365 Quotes from
Women I Love

ANDY COHEN

ANDY COHEN BOOKS   HENRY HOLT AND COMPANY   NEW YORK

Andy Cohen Books
Henry Holt and Company
Publishers since 1866
120 Broadway
New York, New York 10271
www.henryholt.com

Andy Cohen Books® and ◣® are registered trademarks of Macmillan Publishing Group, LLC.

Library of Congress Cataloging-in-Publication data is available.

ISBN:9781250832399

Our books may be purchased in bulk for promotional, educational, or business use. Please contact your local bookseller or the Macmillan Corporate and Premium Sales Department at (800) 221-7945, extension 5442, or by e-mail at MacmillanSpecialMarkets@macmillan.com.

First Edition 2021

Designed by Meryl Sussman Levavi

Printed in the United States of America

1   3   5   7   9   10   8   6   4   2

This book is dedicated to women everywhere.
You run the world!

PREFACE

I'm inspired by women every day of my life. They make me laugh and think and challenge me to be a better human. The inspiration all started with my mom, a powerhouse who always encouraged me to be myself. It continued with Lucy, who not only entertained me on TV, but (as you'll read on October 15) provided me great inspiration in the form of a well-worn library book that had my mother worried I was an airhead (spoiler alert: I was). From there I moved on to the majesty of Diana Ross, who was like a Diva-Superhero, then Madonna, whose music took me to the moon and attitude rocked my soul, and a galaxy of other female icons in the world of entertainment, who dazzled and delighted me. Most of my mentors in my career have been women, and they've seemed to "get" me in a way that others haven't. And then there are the Real Housewives, who give me the daily drama and laughs I've grown to depend on; and without them, I wouldn't be half the man I am today (or have half my gray hair).

My goal with this book is to provide you with a daily meditation unlike those you might find in other books of *actual* daily meditations. I can guarantee that this is a group of women you won't find bundled in any other place, but their quotes will hopefully make you inspired, amused, shocked, think about something differently, or just shake your cage!

Think of each quote as a sparkly cloud of glitter, sprinkled freshly onto each new day!

GLITTER
EVERY DAY

"Get a hold of yourself, Andy!"

—Evelyn Cohen

Whenever my mom says this to me, it's like a slap of reality in my face. This chestnut has been used for years in especially heated moments when she thinks I'm doing something very stupid. Spending too much on needless trifles? *Get a hold of yourself, Andy!* Not going to the doctor when I'm clearly sick? *Get a hold of yourself, Andy!* Living on caffeine and five hours sleep? *Get a hold of yourself, Andy!* Sometimes we all just need a metaphorical slap in the face from our mothers to take stock and get a hold of ourselves!

◊ On the first day of the year, it's important to listen to your mother!

JANUARY

"Everything is right on time."
—Hoda Kotb

I remember pulling Hoda aside at Sirius one day, confiding that Ben was on his way. Hodes was an immediate calming burst of enthusiasm and guiding force when we discussed having kids later in life. She completely put me at ease about every stress running through my mind. Everything is right on time, indeed.

◊ Hoda Kotb was named the co-anchor of *Today* on this date in 2018.

3

JANUARY

"The man who gets me is getting one hell
of a woman."
—Aretha Franklin

Aretha knew she was a prize and acted like one until the day she died. Self-worth is so powerful and one of the greatest things we can pass on to our kids, and I'm praying mine walk through life the way Aretha did.

◇ On this date in 1987, Aretha Franklin became the first woman ever inducted into the Rock & Roll Hall of Fame.

JANUARY

"The fact that I can reproduce is very scary."

—Nicole "Snooki" Polizzi

The fact that Snooki is so self-aware made me less scared about her having kids.

◊ Snooki's first book (she has three!!), *A Shore Thing*, was published on January 4, 2011.

JANUARY

"But how will you know when to wipe me?"

—Kelly Ripa

I played a game on *Watch What Happens Live* with Anderson Cooper, Ripa, and all of our assistants. This was Kelly's response after her assistant said her grossest habit is going to the bathroom with the door open, and it made me laugh for days after she said it. She is so fast and funny, and I love how dirty she gets in my Clubhouse.

◇ Kelly Ripa's last appearance on *All My Children* as Hayley Vaughan aired on this day in 2010, when she returned for the series' fortieth anniversary.

JANUARY

"I regard *Real Housewives* as anthropological documents."
—Camille Paglia

So do I, Camille Paglia! I've been saying for years that the show is like a sociological time capsule of how a certain group of women lived and interacted in different cities. Someday, in a galaxy far, far away, people are going to study this, I'm convinced!

◊ On January 6, 2017, Camille Paglia published the scathing essay on show business "How to Age Disgracefully in Hollywood," trumpeting how to age with grace and class without all the Botox and filler. But do that, too, if it makes you feel good.

JANUARY 7

"Everybody's a little bi."
—Sandra Bernhard

S andy—always a trailblazer, artistically and personally—said this on Arsenio Hall in 1992. Her freedom in expressing her sexuality in that era opened a lot of people's minds.

◊ Today is a good day to explore your bisexuality!

JANUARY

"I don't apologize because I never
make mistakes."
—Tiffany "New York" Pollard

This would be such a brilliant *Housewives* tagline, and it's the perfect attitude for any reality star—unrepentant narcissism in full bloom!

◊ *I Love New York* premiered on VH1 on January 8, 2007.

JANUARY

"I've always walked around and noticed things and other people also used to notice things, but then everyone but me got a phone and so now everyone is just looking at the phone and they've bequeathed the entire city to me."

—Fran Lebowitz

Phones suck, and they're going to kill us all, one way or another. And Fran is lucky to not be involved in any of these phone shenanigans. In summary, these phones are going to kill us all. I'm sorry to ruin your day.

◊ Apple Inc. CEO Steve Jobs announced the iPhone on this date in 2007.

JANUARY

"I. Love. Bread. I love bread. I now just manage
it so I don't deny myself bread. I have bread
every day. I have bread every day!"
—Oprah Winfrey

Oprah loves bread! Do you hear me!? Oprah. Loves. Bread. She has it
every day!

◇ On this date in 2018, Oprah gave a speech at the Golden Globes that began a short-
lived movement to get her to run for president.

11

JANUARY

"The more you live, the less you die."

—Janis Joplin

While I don't advocate overdosing at the age of twenty-seven, I think Joplin makes a great point. This is one of the reasons I moved to New York City: *to live.* I always appreciate the idea that anyone could drop by at any time, or I might be summoned for a late-night drink by a friend who happens to be in the neighborhood.

Living > Sleep

◊ Janis Joplin's second and final solo studio album, *Pearl*, was released posthumously on January 11, 1971.

12 JANUARY

"The body is like a car: the older you become,
the more care you have to take care of it—and
you don't leave a Ferrari out in the sun."

—Joan Collins

I was over for lunch at Collins's Saint-Tropez house in the early aughts, and she was indeed very protected from the sun! Even better, she looked like a Ferrari!

◊ *Dynasty* premiered on this date in 1981.

13 JANUARY

"I beat Meryl!"

—Jennifer Lawrence

I love people who say what they think, and if I beat Meryl Streep, I'd probably shout it from the rooftops, too.

◊ Jennifer Lawrence made this remark while accepting a Golden Globe on this date in 2013.

"Keepin' it hot!"

—Natasha Richardson

This is something Natasha and I started saying to our group of friends as a joke, but it actually became a bit of a mantra for us. A paparazzi photo ran of Natasha and Liam Neeson kissing on a beach with the wildly cheesy headline "Keepin' It Hot!" We'd laughingly use every opportunity to headline any mundane activity with "Keepin' it hot!" but the expression morphed into us challenging each other to essentially keep the proverbial party going.

◊ Natasha Richardson made her Broadway debut in the play *Anna Christie* on January 14, 1993. This was also where she met her future husband, Liam Neeson.

JANUARY

"I do think it's smart to see a [marriage] as
'a garden and a gardener who constantly swap
roles.' You really have to switch
from one to another."

—Carla Bruni

Leave it to the former First Lady of France to remind us that we all need to be versatile with our partners, and this applies to gay men who say they're "strictly tops." (If I'm confusing you, call your gay bestie, and he'll explain.)

◊ Carla Bruni released her second studio album, *No Promises*, on January 15, 2007.

JANUARY

"There are seven drag performers in Las Vegas,
right now, doing me."
—Carol Channing

I was gonna say there's no bigger honor than being impersonated by seven drag queens, but then Carol said in the same 1996 interview (with Conan O'Brien) that "[she] was made a honorary lesbian." I don't know what any of that means, but it sounds hilarious and something to be very proud of!

◊ *Hello, Dolly!* opened on Broadway on January 16, 1964. Carol Channing won a Tony for Best Actress in a Musical for playing Dolly.

"Every now and then it helps to be a little
deaf . . . That advice has stood me in good
stead. Not simply in dealing with my marriage,
but in dealing with my colleagues."
—Justice Ruth Bader Ginsburg

Isn't that wise? If we can all tune out some of the bullshit—from online trolls, critics, husbands, annoying people at work, then we won't take it on, and it'll remain nonsense. It's up to each of us to decide whether we need to hear every damn thing. (We don't!)

◊ Ruth Bader Ginsburg argued her first case before the Supreme Court on January 17, 1973. The Court decided in *Frontiero v. Richardson* that the United States military could not give out benefits to the families of service members differently because of their sex.

18 JANUARY

"I don't believe in marriage because I don't believe in divorce. If I had been married, I would have been divorced about five or six times already."

—Grace Jones

I never understood some people's obsession with marriage. I think this is an entirely reasonable attitude and would've probably served a lot of people well.

◊ On this day in 1996, Lisa Marie Presley filed for divorce from Michael Jackson. She should've listened to Grace!

JANUARY

"The audacity to judge someone's natural-ass face when literally none of us chose our natural faces will always escape me."

—Robin Thede

As someone who peddles in the trade of women who mess with their faces, somehow this God-given POV has previously escaped me!

◊ Robin Thede became the first Black woman to be the head writer of a late-night show. *The Nightly Show with Larry Wilmore* premiered on Comedy Central on January 19, 2015.

JANUARY

"Optimism is the fuel driving every fight
I've been in."
—Kamala Harris

Something I have in common with the VP! Optimism (and passion) are the fuel for how I try to view things professionally and personally. (BE-REAL ALERT: I can be an absolute Negative Nellie and Pain in the Ass, too.) It's pretty clear that putting a positive spin on things, or seeing something from another point of view, makes everything better. It doesn't always work, but it's a great mantra.

◊ Kamala Harris was sworn in as the first woman, Black person, and South Asian American vice president of the United States of America on January 20, 2021.

21 JANUARY

"It's selfish, but I think the word 'selfish' gets
a bad rap."
—Sarah Paulson

This is Paulson commenting on dedicating herself to her career and not having kids, which I wouldn't call selfish. I'd say it's commendable that she's living her own truth. It's her life to live the way she wants.

◊ Today is a great day to treat yourself!

22

JANUARY

"Youthfulness is connected to the ability to see things new for the first time. So if your eyes still look at life with wonder, then you will seem young, even though you may not be chronologically young."

—Goldie Hawn

The sun truly shines from within Goldie, and now we know it's because she looks at everything like a newborn from those great big eyes! May we all have Goldie's vision (and legs).

◊ Goldie Hawn's first big break was on the *Rowan & Martin's Laugh-In* sketch show that premiered on NBC on January 22, 1968.

"I think through anything difficult in life, you have a choice to either make you bitter or better."

—Marie Osmond

I grew up on the wholesome goodness of *Donny & Marie*, a '70s vibe capsule drenched in synchronized saccharine. It was a sweet way to learn that bitter is never a good taste in your mouth. I feel like if we all lived in Osmondland, bitter would be obsolete.

◇ The *Donny & Marie* variety show premiered on ABC on January 23, 1976.

"My career's not my life. It's my hobby."
—Adele

If one of the greatest singers in the world saying this isn't enough to get you off the computer and onto the floor playing board games with your kids, I don't know what will. (Actually, I do: Listen to "Cat's in the Cradle" and then let's talk.)

◊ Adele's second album, *21*, was released on January 24, 2011, and is still the best-selling album of the twenty-first century with over 30 million copies sold.

JANUARY

"Am I the greatest? I don't know.
I'm the greatest that I can be."

—Serena Williams

I always admire the strength and tenacity of high achievers who push themselves to be the best they can. I want to be great at tennis, or at least good at tennis, or—let's face it—would like to be able to go hit balls with a friend and wear cute white clothes and then have cocktails in my outfit by the side of the court, but I happen to suck at tennis and invariably give up. Is this the greatest I can be? Possibly.

◊ At the Australian Open on January 25, 2003, Serena Williams achieved the "Serena Slam" when she defeated her sister Venus Williams in a Grand Slam final for the fourth consecutive time.

JANUARY

"Get up on the table and dance for fucking
Andy Cohen and the baby!"

—Lisa Rinna

Suffice to say that my baby shower—which ended with forty Real Housewives dancing on tables at the command of Lisa Rinna—redefined the entire notion of what a baby shower can be! I love a rallying cry to party and celebrate, and Lisa's will live on in memes and in my heart!

◊ Andy's legendary baby shower took place on January 26, 2019.

"No, no, no, Oprah! Whitney don't cook!"

—Whitney Houston

There's a lot to love here. First of all, I always loved when Whitney referred to herself in the third person, as she did on *Oprah* when asked about her cooking. The larger point is that Whitney didn't need to cook. When you're the GOAT, just do what you're best at, and let everybody else fill in the blanks.

◇ Whitney Houston performed the national anthem at the Super Bowl on this date in 1991.

JANUARY

"I think it's important that young people
recognize the value of the elders in their lives
and to take advantage of their presence while
they are still there."

—Cicely Tyson

Grab your grandma and a tape recorder and hit record, kids. Listen to
their stories, and take notes. Not paying due to one's elders is not only
bad manners, it's stupid.

◊ Cicely Tyson died at the age of ninety-six on January 28, 2021.

JANUARY

"Don't carry weed in your vagina or black out."
—Ilana Glazer

If you came to this book looking for some practical advice, it's safe to say my work is done thanks to Ilana Glazer.

◊ Drink a lot of water today, and every day!

JANUARY 30

"When you're an outsider or a misfit, if you play
it smart, your motto should be, 'I'll show 'em.
I will show you.'"
—Wendy Williams

Whether you're "too tall," or "too weird," or "too gay," use the quality
that makes you stand out to your advantage. Side note: Misfits are often
the most fun people to hang out with.

◊ Wendy Williams's infamous radio interview with Whitney Houston aired on January 30, 2003.

JANUARY 31

"You can tell how smart people are by
what they laugh at."

—Tina Fey

My best indication for how a first date is going, and whether I see potential in a guy, is if we laugh at the same thing. Every guy I've ever crushed on has shared my love for shows like *The Comeback*, *SCTV*, and *Kath & Kim*.

◊ The *30 Rock* series finale aired on January 31, 2013.

"Don't tell girls they can be anything they want when they grow up. Because it would have never occurred to them that they couldn't. It's like saying, 'Hey, when you get in the shower, I'm not gonna read your diary.' 'Wait—are you gonna read my diary?' 'No! I said I'm not gonna read your diary. Go take a shower!'"

—Sarah Silverman

This is a brilliant way of looking at something (girls can do anything!) that I might've otherwise thought worthy of including in this book. Don't even say it. Just live it!

◊ *The Sarah Silverman Program* premiered on Comedy Central on February 1, 2007.

FEBRUARY

"I majored in art history in college. So that is
kind of what I saw myself doing."

—Farrah Fawcett

If you had three guesses of what Farrah Fawcett majored in in college,
I am pretty sure that art history would not be one of them! This just
goes to show you that a college major does not predetermine your life.
Let's be real. I'm sure art historians enjoy showing people around art
museums, but Farrah went a step beyond her major and *became* art!

◊ On February 2, 2011, Farrah Fawcett's famous red swimsuit and an original copy of
  the poster of her in the suit were enshrined in the Smithsonian Institution's National
  Museum of American History.

"For a long time . . . I defined myself by what
I wasn't, which constantly set me up for failure
and disappointment. And my life changed
when I focused on what I was good at,
what I liked most about myself,
and what made me stand out."

—Issa Rae

As Jerri Blank (one of my favorite fictional idiots) put it: "Go with what you KNOW!"

° Issa Rae's web series *The Misadventures of Awkward Black Girl* premiered on February 3, 2011.

4 FEBRUARY

"There is always magic to be summoned at any point. I love to live in a world of magic, but not a fake world of magic. We all really basically have a lot of magic . . . it's only those of us that choose to accept it that really understand it. It's there for everyone."

—Stevie Nicks

I like to picture Stevie on any given night twisting in circles amidst gauzy crepe and candlelight, with the faint sound of wind chimes in the distance and patchouli wafting through the air. I'd like to say that I, like Stevie, live in a world of magic, but I'd be bullshitting you. But I appreciate those who do and wish I could.

◊ Fleetwood Mac's *Rumours* album was released on February 4, 1977.

FEBRUARY

"Life isn't all diamonds and rosé . . .
but it should be."

—Lisa Vanderpump

One of the iconic *Housewives* taglines from someone who quite literally lives surrounded by diamonds and rosé. When you go to LVP's house—and I hope you all do at some point in your life—you will see that what you see on TV is Lisa's reality. If you can manifest this reality, make it happen!

◊ Lisa Vanderpump plays the leading lady in the music video for ABC's "Poison Arrow." The song was released in the United Kingdom on February 5, 1982.

FEBRUARY

"If you can't be better than your competition,
just dress better."

—Anna Wintour

Doesn't dressing "up" make you feel better about yourself? Put on something you love today. Do it for Anna!

◊ Wear something outrageous today and tweet me a picture of your outfit. I dare you . . .

GLITTER EVERY DAY   37

FEBRUARY

"Beauty fades, dumb is forever."
—Judy Sheindlin

There's no way Judy came up with this line, but it was the title of one of her books, it's true, and I don't wanna make no trouble with JJ, so I'm gonna go ahead and attribute it to her.

◇ Judy Sheindlin's first of several books, *Don't Pee on My Leg and Tell Me It's Raining*, came out on February 7, 1996. I'm not sure she made up that quote either, but what do I know?!

8

FEBRUARY

"I moved my whole family . . . I bought
[my mom] a house, bought her a mink coat.
I did everything, retired her. I did everything
I ever promised her."

—Ja'Net DuBois

I loved Willona on *Good Times*, and I love that Ja'Net DuBois proudly represented the "I got rich and bought my whole family houses" trope. This is what everybody's fantasy is of hitting it rich, and she did it!

◊ *Good Times* premiered on February 8, 1974.

9 FEBRUARY

"If you want to be a writer, stop talking about it
and sit down and write!"

—Jackie Collins

The hardest thing about writing is sitting down and actually doing it. Once you know your voice and actually start going, it becomes easier and easier. Jump off the bridge and do it!

◊ Jackie Collins's twenty-seventh novel, *Poor Little Bitch Girl* (how amazing is that title?), was published in the United States on February 9, 2010.

"I feel so nervous. My stomach been hurting.
I've been farting all day."

—Cardi B

Finally someone on a red carpet says what everyone else is thinking!!!
Keeping it real always wins my heart.

◊ Cardi B became the only woman to win a Grammy for Best Rap Album as a solo
artist, on February 10, 2019.

FEBRUARY 11

"If this show's a success, then I'm going to learn to love that 'female dog.'"
—Vivian Vance

This is TAFKAE (The Artist Formerly Known As Ethel) reminiscing that Lucille Ball was brutally cold to her at their first meeting, leading Vance to look at the big picture *and* gracefully find other words to call Lucy a bitch in the process. How wise of her to play the long game, because I'd say it worked out pretty well for both of them; they wound up working together for the rest of their lives and becoming great pals.

◊ Vivian Vance became the very first person to win an Emmy for Best Supporting Actress, on this day in 1954!

12

FEBRUARY

"You better check your lipstick before you
come and talk to me."
—Naomi Campbell

Will do, Naomi! And I'm gonna expand that thought to recommend checking your breath before seeing anyone of note, as well, especially Naomi. Bad breath is my absolute pet peeve, and the thing that gets me walking backwards for the exit. I live in fear of it. I also live in fear of walking into, say, Naomi Campbell's dressing room and having something messed up with my face (a zit??) or breath. So pretend every door has Naomi on the other side of it and: Deal with your lips and breath, people!

◊ Buy a bunch of breath mints today and place them strategically in your car, office, and home!

FEBRUARY 13

"I just love bossy women. I could be around them all day. To me, bossy is not a pejorative term at all. It means somebody's passionate and engaged and ambitious and doesn't mind leading."

—Amy Poehler

What some call bossy, I call alluring! I gravitate to strong women. From my mother, to bosses and mentors I've had along the way, to the Housewives, I find women who are firmly in charge totally captivating. Find yourself a man who appreciates a woman in command, and you've found a great man.

◊ Happy Galentine's Day! This holiday originated from an episode of *Parks and Recreation* and quickly became a "holiday" meant for ladies to celebrate fellow ladies.

14 FEBRUARY

"I found that the worse you make them feel, the better after that they know how to do it better."

—Nicki Minaj

This is Nicki explaining to Ellen DeGeneres that women can't be afraid to tell men when they're not satisfying them. Queen Nicki advises shaming them so they never make the same mistake again. I think it's a daring proposition, and it'll either work, or the man will never achieve another erection.

◇ Nicki Minaj's song "Starships" was released on this day in 2012. Happy Valentine's Day!

15
FEBRUARY

"I've learned that people will forget what you said, people will forget what you did, but people will never forget how you made them feel."

—Maya Angelou

This is a lesson for the ages, for all ages, and one that I've already imparted to my son and will continue to impart forever. Sometimes at the end of the day, a moment will hit me when I'll realize that I could've done better, and it's often a painful realization to think you've hurt someone else. Seeing feelings painted so vividly on my son's face is a great reminder of the most basic thing we should all remember as we navigate our days encountering other humans. Everybody has feelings!

◊ Maya Angelou received the Presidential Medal of Freedom on February 15, 2011.

16

FEBRUARY

"Drama is very important in life: You have to come on with a bang. You never want to go out with a whimper. Everything can have drama if it's done right. Even a pancake."

—Julia Child

A pancake, you say!? I agree! Drama is the essence of fun for me, and I do anything to lean into the drama of an otherwise mundane event—a meal, an errand, a walk with a friend. Once, at dinner with my family, I announced that Richard Nixon had died; he was very much alive, but I wanted to see how my parents would react. (They were momentarily shocked, then spent fifteen minutes trying to figure out why I did it.) Suffice to say I'm in the right line of work.

◊ Happy National Pancake Day!

FEBRUARY 17

"The great thing about McDonald's is that they have a lot of different things on the menu. I love their salads."

—Beyoncé

Beyoncé said this many years ago in defense of Destiny's Child's contract with McDonald's. I personally haven't deviated from my childhood order of two cheeseburgers and fries, but I appreciate Bey's optimism about the McDonald's menu and commitment to being a good corporate citizen!

◊ Destiny's Child's self-titled debut album, "No, No, No," was released in the United States on this day in 1998.

18
FEBRUARY

"I, like many of us, was taught to grow up dreaming of my wedding not of my life. And I spent many years dreaming of my wedding and also waiting to be chosen. Well, here's the thing. I'm the chooser and I can choose to get married if I want to, but in the meantime, I am choicefully single, happily, gloriously single."

—Tracee Ellis Ross

Tracee knows—and celebrates—who she is. I love and respect that. I also have a feeling she has pets because pets make us feel like we're not alone.

◊ Tracee Ellis Ross's first role in a major studio film was in the film *Hanging Up,* which was released on February 18, 2000.

"And I have been in this business for twenty
years and I'm still here. I'm still here and
I'm still fabulous. Right? Fabulous!
Gone with the Wind fabulous!"

—Kenya Moore

I'm still not sure what *"Gone with the Wind* fabulous" actually means,
but it sounds great and became truly infamous after Beyoncé quoted
Kenya as she walked away from her Super Bowl Halftime Show in 2013.

◊ Kenya Moore won the Miss USA pageant on this day in 1993.

20 FEBRUARY

"I'm tired of people not treating me like
the gift that I am."
—Paula Abdul

Besides giving the *Bratz* movie a bigger platform than it deserved, Paula Abdul's short-lived reality show *Hey Paula* gave us Paula delivering this line in all seriousness. And she is a gift.

◊ "Forever Your Girl" was released on this day in 1989.

"You're the sum total of the five people you
spend the most time with.
Choose your friends wisely."
—Hoda Kotb

Hodes is giving me something to think about here! By her logic, as
I write this (in the tail end of the pandemic), I'm most like: my son,
his nanny, my executive producer, my doorman, and my trainer Stanny.
This makes me highly productive and in shape, with a dependence on
a sippy cup and a tendency to poop my pants but an ability to change
my own diapers and remember a lot of names. This exercise is fun but
might work better when there's no pandemic!

◊ On February 21, 2017, Hoda announced on *Today* that she had adopted a baby girl.

22

FEBRUARY

"I married a guy that is good-looking, but I married because he also have a lot of money."
—Charo

Three points to Charo for her honesty!!! (I'm glad the guy was good-looking because it softens the blow of marrying for money.)

◊ Make friends with a rich person today! Maybe they'll buy you something.

"Well, I met Sandy Bullock at an awards thing a couple years ago, and she said to me, 'If I were gay, you'd be the one.' And I said, 'I'm there!'"

—Emma Thompson

Sandra Bernhard did say that "everyone's bi," so it's a good idea to figure out who your type is if it ever comes up!

◊ Emma Thompson wrote and starred in the Academy Award–winning film *Sense and Sensibility*, which premiered in the UK on February 23, 1996. The film won the Oscar for Best Adapted Screenplay, making Emma the only person to have won Oscars for both acting and screenwriting.

24 FEBRUARY

"Some people think having large breasts makes a woman stupid. Actually, it's quite the opposite: a woman having large breasts makes men stupid."

—Rita Rudner

Confession: As gay as I am (and I'm as gay as a beaded handbag), even I remain powerless to the allure of large breasts. They make me stupid, too! No matter your sexuality, I believe we all must acknowledge the wonder and glory of the bosom. How do you think I stay so entertained for hours on end taping *Housewives* reunions? I'm just transfixed by the bounty before me!

◊ Dolly Parton won a Grammy for Best Country Song and Best Female Country Vocal Performance on this day in 1982.

"I have never savored life with such gusto
as I do now."

—Candice Bergen

As Bevy Smith says, "It gets greater, later," and Bergen seems to embody that sentiment. I interviewed her several times during the *Murphy Brown* era, and she didn't seem, how can I put this, very happy. (Just my dime-store opinion!) Conversely, in the ten times I've spoken to her in the last decade, she has seemed absolutely ebullient. Not sure what happened, but I love that evolution.

◊ Today might be the day to start binging *Murphy Brown*.

"No, I don't have to give this back.
It's got my name on it!"

—Halle Berry

There are very few movie stars who can win an Oscar and then show up to the Razzies (which celebrate the worst in film) to accept an award for Worst Actress *while holding her Oscar*. Halle Berry proved it's better to put ego aside and laugh at yourself when you make a mistake. She not only walked onstage (to accept her award for *Catwoman*) holding her Oscar, but she also mimicked her famous mouth-gaping cry that she did when she made history as the first Black woman to win Best Actress at the Academy Awards (for *Monster's Ball*)! Halle reclaimed the narrative and laughed at herself and admitted that she should've listened to her gut when making a movie she knew would be terrible.

◊ Halle Berry accepted her Razzie Award for Worst Actress on February 26, 2005.

FEBRUARY 27

"Be cool . . . don't be all, like, uncool."

—Countess Luann

When Luann de Lesseps said this now-infamous line in season 7 of *The Real Housewives of New York City*, wearing a bikini, robe, and massive sunglasses, it ushered in a whole new Lu. The etiquette-obsessed countess was replaced by a blowsy, freewheeling broad. It became one of the most GIFed moments in all the *Housewives*, and a mantra to chill the f out.

◊ The first show of #CountessandFriends debuted at Feinstein's/54 Below on this day in 2018. Theater history!

28 FEBRUARY

"There should be a party on your foot no matter
the height of the shoe."
—Sarah Jessica Parker

This is a lady who's always hosting a rager on her feet. She literally walks her talk.

◇ The SJP Collection by Sarah Jessica Parker officially launched on this day in 2014.

"We've begun to raise daughters more like sons, but few have the courage to raise our sons more like our daughters."

—Gloria Steinem

I loved this before, and love it even more as a dad.

◊ March 1 is the start of Women's History Month.

MARCH

"My agent said, 'You aren't good enough for movies.' I said, 'You're fired.'"
—Sally Field

There's a lot to unpack here, because I do marvel at an agent honest (and dumb?) enough to say they don't see movies in Sally's future. But Sally wins by knowing what she wants, believing in herself, and having the strength to dump someone who doesn't tell her what she needs to hear.

◊ *Norma Rae* was released in the United States on March 2, 1979.

3

MARCH

"If I have learned anything it is that you cannot run away from who you are or from how you've been shaped by your experiences. Instead, you must integrate your past and present."

—Monica Lewinsky

Monica is a brilliant example of how to grow into oneself.

[◊] Monica Lewinsky's famous interview with Barbara Walters aired on this day in 1999, and was watched by 70 million people.

4

MARCH

"A woman is like a tea bag. You never know
how strong it is until it's in hot water."
—Eleanor Roosevelt

There is some question about whether Eleanor Roosevelt actually said this, but Hillary Clinton quoted it in the *New York Times*, so I'm gonna go with it. I love the sentiment, I love women, and I love tea!

◇ Eleanor Roosevelt became the First Lady of the United States on March 4, 1933.

"Kim, there's people that are dying."

—Kourtney Kardashian

Kourtney Kardashian tried to keep things perfectly in perspective as her sister Kim sobbed after being thrown in the ocean and losing one of her $75,000 earrings on an episode of *Keeping Up with the Kardashians*.

◊ Kourtney Kardashian launched her lifestyle website, Poosh, on this day in 2019.

6

MARCH

"At the end of your life, you will never regret not having passed one more test, winning one more verdict, or not closing one more deal. You will regret time not spent with a husband, a child, a friend, or a parent."

—Barbara Bush

"And the cat's in the cradle and the silver spoon." Sorry I digress, but that song really does overcome me with melancholy. Barbara shares a similar sentiment without making me want to poop.

◊ Barbara Bush launched the Barbara Bush Foundation for Family Literacy on March 6, 1989.

7

MARCH

"Our culture is set up on a feud mentality, or a 'Housewives' mentality, that women just fight. And it's such a shallow way to exist as far as our evolution is concerned, and our culture is concerned. It's fun to watch women fight, in a storytelling way, but in the *world*, women shouldn't be seen as a threat to other women."

—Laura Linney

✧

Though I contribute and often delight in that mentality, I'd first like to point out that the *Real Housewives*, the show, actually brings women together. It's something they can have fun talking about and laughing with. It's worth noting that if the show was only feuding, we wouldn't be talking about it sixteen years into its run. It has heart and humor, just like the women who watch. OK, let me get off my soapbox and agree that women shouldn't be seen as a threat to other women!

◇ Laura Linney co-starred in the 2002 revival of *The Crucible* that opened on Broadway on March 7, 2002. I was lucky enough to be in the audience!

8 MARCH

"You deserve to feel Good As Hell,
we deserve to feel Good As Hell."

—Lizzo

Good As Hell = You at your best, most self-confident. I love Lizzo's attitude, bravery, and all-around fierceness; after all, she went from working in a tax office to being "that bitch."

◊ Lizzo's single "Good as Hell" was released on this day in 2016.

MARCH 9

"What is a frappuccino going to lead to?
A piggyback ride? No!"
—Chelsea Handler

I absolutely hate coffee dates, too! My go-to first date is a cocktail. And if I'm mildly into the guy, I have a second. And if I have a second, I invariably walk away from the date thinking it went way better than it did and that he was cuter than he was. And all this leads me to wonder if I'm wrong about coffee dates. Sorry for wasting your time.

◇ Chelsea Handler's book of comedic essays, *Chelsea Chelsea Bang Bang*, was published on March 9, 2010.

10 MARCH

"I thought [my face] was hideous. I couldn't stand it! Well, now I'm a great many years older and I see some of those films and I don't think there is any question I was the best-looking woman ever in film."

—Bette Davis

I learned this lesson when I once asked Diane von Furstenberg to take some thirst-trappy pics of me on a Jet Ski. I grimaced as I looked through them. "You'll love them in seven years," she said. I never forgot that.

◇ Bette Davis's film *Jezebel* came out on this day in 1938.

11

MARCH

"When your children are teenagers,
it's important to have a dog so that someone
in the house is happy to see you."
—Nora Ephron

I never felt more loved than when I had a dog, and it was amazing how much emotional satisfaction I got from our relationship.

◊ Hug a dog today!

MARCH

"I got your number, hussy."

—Dionne Warwick

Dionne Warwick said this on *Celebrity Apprentice* to Niki Taylor, and it began the era of the more uncensored version of the always classy chanteuse. Also, I'd like to note that if Dionne Warwick ever called me a hussy, or told me she had my number, I'd poop my pants.

◇ Dionne Warwick won her first Grammy on this day in 1969.

MARCH

"And at the end of the day, funny and interesting
will always kick pretty and perfect's ass."

—Kristen Johnston

This is the simple truth. I was once seated at the Met Ball across from a couple that's envied around the world for their beauty, and they essentially lulled me to sleep with their pulse-slowing banter. How could a couple so beautiful on the outside be full of cardboard under the wrapper? Give me funny or give me death!

◊ Kristen Johnston's book, *Guts: The Endless Follies and Tiny Triumphs of a Giant Disaster*, was published on March 13, 2012.

14

MARCH

"I just don't feel that my algebra teacher should
ever know what my butt looks like."

—Julia Roberts

Roberts was discussing why she doesn't do nude scenes, but I'd further this great point to include editing posts on social media as well. Regarding the nudes, if I ever have the opportunity to chat with Julia Roberts, I might debate whether she might've had one algebra teacher whose ass she *did* want to see. If so, maybe we should give people an occasional peek of our asses so they'll pay it forward and show us theirs. Just spitballing . . .

◊ *Erin Brockovich* was released on this day in 2000. Roberts won the Oscar for Best Actress for the title role. March 14 also happens to be Pi Day—a famous math holiday!

MARCH

"The body is meant to be seen,
not all covered up."
—Marilyn Monroe

Hell yes, it is, Marilyn—and tell that to Julia Roberts, who's worried about her algebra teacher seeing her ass! I respect body positivity and other people's right to share theirs!

◇ In March of 1952, Monroe was embroiled in a scandal when she revealed she'd posed for a nude calendar a few years earlier, proving she meant what she said about seeing bodies!

16
MARCH

"You don't learn from successes; you don't learn
from awards; you don't learn from celebrity;
you only learn from wounds and scars and
mistakes and failures. And that's the truth."
—Jane Fonda

I learned this one from one of my mentors, Lauren Zalaznick. When she hired me to run production for Bravo, the first show I produced was *Battle of the Network Reality Stars*, a twist on the '80s phenomenon. I was SURE it was going to be a huge hit. It flopped. Lauren commissioned research to figure out why it didn't work. We discovered it was off-brand and on the wrong network. The ratings estimates, had it aired on E! or VH1, were much higher. Good to know! It's also really important to learn how to handle failure and success. (It's more fun to learn how to handle success.)

◇ *The China Syndrome* was released theatrically on March 16, 1979.

17 MARCH

"In my community of Harlem, thick thighs have always saved lives, so why should I apologize or shroud myself in a muumuu because I've gained weight? I wasn't going to put my dreams on layaway until I could fit a sample size. America was going to have to learn to love (or at least accept) my curves on their TV screens."

—Bevy Smith

Bevy is not only a wordsmith; she's a role model for accentuating what you've got. I knew from the moment I met her that we'd work together, and though it took a minute, I'm happy to say we've collaborated in several mediums.

◇ Bevy Smith's show *Fashion Queens* premiered on Bravo on this day in 2013.

18 MARCH

"Whenever you want to marry someone, go have lunch with his ex-wife."

—Shelley Winters

This is the best advice in the book.

◊ *The Diary of Anne Frank* was released on March 18, 1959. Winters won Best Supporting Actress at the Academy Awards for her role as Mrs. Van Daan.

MARCH

"It's so important to raise people to grow up
to be who they are and not be forced to be
who they're not. What an awful thing to do to
people—it's like being in prison."

—Marlo Thomas

Save this quote for someone trying to understand someone who just
came out to them. It pretty much says it all. Striving to remove whatever metaphorical prison walls are around us is a long construction
project we should never stop working on.

◊ The series finale of *That Girl* aired on March 19, 1971.

MARCH

"BRAVO, BRAVO, FUCKING BRAVO"
—Denise Richards

Richards thought saying this in front of cameras would allow her to break the fourth wall and essentially shut down production. That wasn't the case, and the line inadvertently became something of a catchphrase. Scream it whenever you want to escape your reality and see what happens!

◊ *Wild Things* was released in the United States on March 20, 1998.

MARCH 21

"Let's whoop it up!"

—Vicki Gunvalson

This rallying cry that Vicki used to start the fun bus with her friends in the O.C. has become a mantra for partying that applies to all generations. We should all "Whoop it up" as much as we can, every day.

◊ *The Real Housewives of Orange County* premiered on March 21, 2006.

22 MARCH

"My dream had always been to live a man's life
in a woman's body, and I did it."

—Diane von Furstenberg

I've talked to DVF a lot about her views on sexuality—and her years at Studio 54—and can attest that she has taken ownership and command of herself in a way that I wish more women did; she's unapologetic, fierce, and strong. Why does that have to be a man thing, anyway?

◇ Two years after she introduced the "wrap dress," Diane von Furstenberg appeared on the cover of *Newsweek* on this day in 1976. The corresponding article called her "the most marketable woman since Coco Chanel."

23 MARCH

"I don't like being too looked up at or too looked down on. I prefer meeting in the middle to being worshiped or spat out."

—Joni Mitchell

Joni happens to be a goddess, but I understand that walking in her shoes could be exhausting because of the way people approach her. I'm amazed by the way people lose their shit around famous people, often becoming an alternate (worse) version of themselves. I've done it, too, by the way. (Ask Susan Lucci. Or Madonna.) So take it from me and Joni: If you want to make an impact on a famous person, treat them like a human being.

◊ On March 23, 1968, Joni Mitchell released her debut album, *Song to a Seagull*.

MARCH

"Your lady part is not making history."

—Dr. Jackie Walters

Y ou may *think* your vagina is making history, but think again. I love a doctor who is nonplussed; that's their job. And Dr. Jackie takes that to another level as she reminds us all to communicate with our doctors about our issues—we aren't the first ones experiencing them, and we shouldn't be ashamed.

◊ *Married to Medicine* premiered on Bravo on this day in 2013.

MARCH 25

"I don't look like Halle Berry. But chances are,
she's going to end up looking like me."
—Whoopi Goldberg

I don't look like Halle Berry either, and she sure as hell isn't going to end up looking like me; but Timothée Chalamet will! Wait, is that a stretch? OK . . . I don't look like Darren Criss, but he's going to end up looking like me. Is that a little more in the ballpark? In any case, Whoopi is right on, and this is a comforting thought for everyone who isn't Halle, Timothée, or Darren.

◊ Whoopi Goldberg became the first Black actress to win an Oscar in fifty years when she won Best Supporting Actress for her performance in *Ghost* on this day in 1991.

26
MARCH

"The road to hell is paved with good intentions."
—Evelyn Cohen

◇

I cannot credit my mom with inventing this quote—it goes back hundreds of years—but she says it enough for me to attach it to her. It's the perfect piece of motherly guilt anytime I don't follow through with something, which is not often because I'm a follow-through kind of son. Wait, do I follow through on things because this slam packs such a wallop?

◇ This is a great day to call someone in your family and tell them you love and appreciate them!

27
MARCH

"I don't count years, but I definitely rebuke them.
I have anniversaries, not birthdays, because I
celebrate life, darling."

—Mariah Carey

Mariah ain't kidding when she says she celebrates her "anniversary" instead of her actual birthday, and isn't that grand? *She rebukes years!* As someone who hates the song "Happy Birthday" (to me, it often sounds like a molasses-soaked funeral march), this is a life-changing new approach to aging that I would encourage us all to adopt.

◊ Happy "anniversary," Mariah Carey! On March 27, 1969, Mariah Carey was born.

MARCH 28

"I'm a badass bitch because I've been
farting wherever."

—Ilana Glazer

If you fart everywhere, does that make you incredibly confident, self-ish, or a little of both? I would hold a fart in all day if I was around people, so I don't share Glazer's brazenness, but it's a way of life that gave me cause for pause.

⬦ The series finale of *Broad City* aired on Comedy Central on this day in 2019.

29 MARCH

"I have a personality defect where I refuse to see myself as an underdog."

—Mindy Kaling

That's a defect I can get behind. I also salute Mindy Kaling for: a) having the name "Mindy," which I love, and b) being absolutely hilarious and fearless.

◊ Mindy Kaling's first episode of *The Office* as "Kelly Kapoor" aired on March 29, 2005.

30

MARCH

"Is this chicken, what I have, or is this fish?"

—Jessica Simpson

Embrace your stupidity, folks. Sometimes it can make you a pop culture phenom and earn you millions!

◊ The series finale of *Newlyweds: Nick and Jessica* aired on MTV on March 30, 2005.

31 MARCH

"At the end of the day, we have to remember that bathroom access really is not about bathrooms."

—Laverne Cox

Often, when politicians and commentators pick social issues to fear-monger about, they are really trying to undermine the validity of the very existence of human beings. Decades ago, same-sex marriage was used to divide Americans and portray gay people as undeserving of this equal right because their "lifestyle was a choice." Now, transgender men and women are under attack because some people refuse to open up their minds. You've heard it before; people fear what they do not understand.

◊ Happy International Transgender Day of Visibility!

"We're going to Hooters!"

—Fortune Feimster

Can you think of a better way for a mom to react to her daughter coming out of the closet? And don't you wish a camera crew had captured that visit to the booby bacchanalia? Moms, take note!

◊ Hooters was founded on April 1, 1983, in Clearwater, Florida.

APRIL

"I am a marvelous housekeeper. Every time I
leave a man I keep his house."

—Zsa Zsa Gabor

Before Paris and Nicky Hilton, there were Zsa Zsa and Eva Gabor. They were actresses, of a sort, but they were more famous for being famous than anything else. I met Zsa Zsa when I was the greeter in the *CBS This Morning* greenroom in the early '90s. It was an older, more zaftig model of Zsa Zsa than I expected, but her wit and humor were intact. I even got a photo!

◇ Zsa Zsa Gabor's divorce from George Sanders, her third of seven (not including her annulment in 1983), was finalized on April 2, 1954.

3

APRIL

"Trying to get Ramona laid is like *Saving Private Ryan*. We're all gonna die trying."

—Bethenny Frankel

But at least the war will be fun, with a great reward at the end, Bethenny!

◇ April is National Poetry Month; for *Housewives* fans, Bethenny Frankel is their poet laureate!

APRIL 4

"I absolutely refuse to reveal my age.
What am I—a car?"
—Cyndi Lauper

If she were a car, I like to think Cyndi would be some brightly colored Cadillac. As she points out here, she is absolutely NOT a car, so the discussion is moot. The point is that, like Cyndi, none of us need reveal our ages. It's no one's business and ultimately unimportant in the grand scheme of who we are. That being said, I wear my age as a badge of honor. I've gotten this far, and I'm proud of it. And the alternative is dreadful. But you do you.

◇ Cyndi Lauper wrote the music and lyrics to *Kinky Boots*, which opened on Broadway on April 4, 2013.

5
APRIL

"Power is having a job where you are allowed
to go to the restroom whenever you want."

—Tina Fey

Power is feeling uninhibited enough to poop at work. And real power is being able to do it whenever you want. (See: my year of being chained to the assignment desk at *CBS News*.)

◊ Tina Fey's book *Bossypants* was published on this day in 2011.

APRIL

"The secret is never too big."

—Ricki Lake

I was as surprised as everybody else when Ricki Lake went on TV in 2021 to confess she'd been hiding years of hair loss from everyone around her. None of her friends knew of her secret or the shame she carried around as a result. I can relate: The pain of carrying around the secret of my sexuality until I was twenty could be unbearable, and my lightness after releasing it to the world was a freedom I'd not ever experienced. What a lesson in seeing shame released by just owning it (see: Lisa Rinna)!

◊ *Cry-Baby* was released in the United States on April 6, 1990.

7

APRIL

"A lot of times girls think they're funny,
but they want to be pretty at the same time,
and if you want to be funny, you have to be
willing to get ugly."

—Amy Sedaris

One thing I love about Amy is that she will do anything to her body in order to land a joke. She once spent several days in a fat suit while visiting her father to convince him she'd gained weight because she knew it would annoy him and that he'd appreciate the "reveal" when she let him in on the joke. That's called commitment!

◇ *Strangers with Candy* premiered on Comedy Central on April 7, 1999.

8 APRIL

"Ain't nobody got time for that!"
—Kimberly "Sweet Brown" Wilkins

S weet Brown went viral in 2012 when she said this of an apartment fire in her Oklahoma neighborhood, but you really can apply it to anything and it works! I had her bartend on *WWHL* that year, and she wound up sharing a deep kiss with Shemar Moore after a shotski. The clip is on YouTube, and it's as insane as it sounds!

◊ Sweet Brown went viral on this day in 2012.

APRIL

"HIV does not make people dangerous to know,
so you can shake their hands and give them a
hug. Heaven knows they need it."
—Princess Diana

Diana proved that one hug goes a long way. I can't emphasize enough what an effect Diana's outward affection with AIDS patients had on people's reaction to the disease.

◇ Princess Diana visited London's first AIDS ward at Middlesex Hospital on April 9, 1987.

APRIL

"I hope you live forever, and I never die."

—Emily Rosenfeld

My sister is actually quoting my grandfather here, and it's a beloved toast in my family.

◊ Happy National Siblings Day!

11

APRIL

"I don't give a gnat's ass wrapped around
a rain barrel."

—Mama Dee

Mama Dee is one of the legendary side characters on Bravo, and I find her homespun wisdom completely hilarious and possibly nonsensical! Her hair (wig) is also iconic.

◊ *The Real Housewives of Dallas* premiered on this day in 2016.

12

APRIL

"Always remember: If you're alone in the kitchen and you drop the lamb, you can always just pick it up. Who's going to know?"
—Julia Child

Julia, that's absolutely filthy! Oh well! I always enjoyed what a hot tipsy cheerful mess Julia Child seemed, but it's important to note that she always got that meal together! Julia's joy for life and food has inspired millions, and will for generations to come—so dust off that lamb, and get your shit together!

◊ Julia's second book, *The French Chef Cookbook*, was published on April 12, 1968, and contains the recipes from her TV show.

13 APRIL

"Anybody who says my show is 'neat' has to go."
—Madonna

Put yourself in Madonna's shoes. You've stepped offstage after performing in the Blond Ambition Tour, where you led a troupe of dancers through impeccable choreo, simulated masturbation in an exotic remixed "Like a Virgin," and critiqued the Catholic Church through song, dance, and incredible staging in a show that revolutionized live music for years to come, and Kevin Costner greets you backstage with a one-word review: "Neat!" The moment went the equivalent of viral when *Truth or Dare* was released in 1991, and Madonna later apologized to Costner for sticking her finger down her throat (which was the equivalent in those days of saying "Barf!"). Let's make this a teachable moment: When you're backstage at any show, remember that the performers are looking to hear whatever validates the effort they just made on behalf of the audience (i.e., YOU!). The show is not really over, and you better be prepared to continue worshiping the star who just gave you her all for two hours onstage.

◊ Madonna's Blond Ambition World Tour kicked off in Chiba, Japan, on this day in 1990.

APRIL

"The single best thing about coming out of the closet is that nobody can insult you by telling you what you've just told them."

—Rachel Maddow

I love this twist on a subject I agonized over until I came out at twenty. Years later I worked on *Queer Eye for the Straight Guy*, which turned the word "queer" into something cool.

◇ Rachel Maddow's radio show, *The Rachel Maddow Show*, first aired on April 14, 2005, on the Air America Radio network.

APRIL 15

"Leopard is my neutral."

—Sonja Morgan

This fashion tip should be a way of life!

◇ Sonja Morgan's first episode of *The Real Housewives of New York City* aired on this day in 2010 (season 3, episode 7).

16

APRIL

"Make sure he knows that you're entitled to an orgasm. I like to say it. I'll be like, 'Hey, there are two people here.' I'll be like, 'Oh my God, have you met my clit?' Don't be self-conscious. It's never too late to make new friends—even when that friend is a woman's clitoris."

—Amy Schumer

If I ran for office, one of the things on my platform would be that everyone is entitled to an orgasm. And I'd make it mandatory for all confused straight men to get training in order to make this happen. Orgasms should be like traffic lights or taxes: mandatory and vital to the fabric of society. No one should be able to pretend they don't exist when it doesn't concern them.

◊ Have an orgasm today!

17

APRIL

"When you decide to buck the system, there will be people in your life who won't support you, even though you've always supported them. They will be angry that you're not there the way you were before. They got used to your playing a role in their Lifetime movie, wearing a bad outfit that no longer fits. Isn't it time that you stop playing a supporting role in someone else's life and become the lead in yours?"

—Bevy Smith

If you come into my orbit, chances are you're going to stay there for a long time. I don't recycle friends, but I have had to extricate myself from a couple relationships that were negative impacts on my life. It wasn't easy, but I knew I was doing the right thing. Oh, and while you're getting rid of unsupportive friends, throw out the bad outfit that no longer fits!

◊ Speaking of coming into orbits, on this day in 1970, Apollo 13 safely landed on Earth!

APRIL

"I'm not taking this on."
—June Diane Raphael

June made this phrase popular on the great podcast *Bitch Sesh*, and it's become a life mantra for dealing with stresses of life. When something comes your way that you don't have the tolerance to emotionally onboard, just decide not to take it on. Remain unbothered. Ignore. Delete. Move on.

◊ On this day in 1994, Roseanne Barr and Tom Arnold decided they were through taking each other on, and filed for divorce.

APRIL

19

"I loathe narcissism, but I approve of vanity."
—Diana Vreeland

There is a difference between the two. To me, narcissism means making everything about yourself, while vanity means you keep it right and tight.

◊ On this day in 1960, baseball uniforms began displaying players' names on their backs—both a statement in fashion *and* vanity.

20
APRIL

"Never share a joint with a stranger, even if
they're famous . . . especially if they're
Bill Maher."

—Kathy Bates

I'm not sure I agree with this sentiment because the bragging rights I
now have after getting high (separately) with the likes of Willie Nelson,
Snoop Dogg, Bob Weir, and George R. R. Martin are legendary amongst
my friends. And yes, I just used a Kathy Bates quote to brag to you
about the stellar lineup of people I've joined for a smoke.

◊ Happy 4–20!

"Don't get divorced unless you're really bothered
by the things that don't matter."

—Sarah Jessica Parker

This is great advice and what I might imagine has kept many marriages together. Put things in perspective.

◊ The musical *Annie* opened on Broadway on this date in 1977. Sarah Jessica Parker
  originally played the orphan July before becoming the title character in March 1979.

APRIL

"I changed the Bernice almost as soon as
I heard it."

—Bea Arthur

Bea Arthur knew who she was and who she wasn't from the start!
Between us, I don't love either name.

◊ The series finale of *Maude* aired on CBS on April 22, 1978.

112   ANDY COHEN

"I'm often asked, 'What's your secret to success?' The shorter answer, put in that work. There may be more failures than victories. Yes, I've been blessed to have 24 Grammys, but I've lost 46 times. That meant rejection 46 times. Please don't ever feel entitled to win, just keep working harder. Surrender to the cards you are dealt. It's from that surrender that you get your power. Losing can be the best motivator to get you even bigger wins. So never compare yourself to anyone else."

—Beyoncé

This perfectly illustrates how Beyoncé remains so driven to perfection and hard work. Sometimes rejection, or failure, is just as much—or more—a motivator to succeed. As I think about this quote, I wonder who Beyoncé even could compare herself to. Streisand? Diana Ross? OK, that may be it. (Also, I couldn't let Beyoncé's only quote in this book be about McDonald's!)

◊ Beyoncé's sixth studio album, *Lemonade*, was released on April 23, 2016. As of this writing, she has won a record 28 Grammys!

APRIL

"Here's my rule about shoes, buy them."

—Rachel Zoe

Here's my rule about fashion: Listen to Rachel Zoe.

◊ The series finale of *The Rachel Zoe Project* aired on Bravo on this day in 2013.

APRIL

"It was not a question of whether or not I would be successful, it was a matter of time."

—Donna Summer

I think about Donna Summer's booming, clear, three-octave range often, and lament that she left us way too soon. With the talent she had, of course she knew that it would ultimately reach the masses. I always knew I would have some level of success in television because I was passionate about the medium, great with people, and believed in my abilities. I'm not comparing my TV acumen to Donna Summer's voice, but I believe there's power in knowing what you're good at.

◊ Donna Summer's *Bad Girls* album was released on April 25, 1979.

26

APRIL

"Dear God, please keep my wig on."

—Kim Zolciak-Biermann

How many women have prayed for this very same thing?

◊ *Don't Be Tardy for The Wedding* premiered on this day in 2012.

27 APRIL

"We knew we were different and we wanted to make it OK. But we weren't consciously ever trying to be different, like let's be freaky or shock people. We had this style to amuse ourselves, and we liked to crash parties and wear wigs and just have fun with it."

—Kate Pierson

The B-52's are pure joy—the most unique group that I love. Their sense of fun and style led them to creative heights and fueled their place in music history as the ultimate party band. Their wigs gave them superpowers, and that alone should inspire all of us to fly our flags!

◊ The B-52's third studio album, *Whammy!*, was released on April 27, 1983.

28
APRIL

"I can relate to having those people in your life that you feel are moving on to this great, big, normal life and you're like, 'What's wrong with me?'"

—Kristen Wiig

Amen, Kristen! I graduated from college and immediately began a career in television that's been relentlessly entertaining and time-consuming. I questioned myself for years as friends got married and had kids, and I plowed ahead with my career with my destination set at FUN. I specifically remember reading to a friend's child a bedtime story, with a pit in my stomach, convinced I was doing it all wrong and wouldn't have a chance at a conventional family. But going at my own speed in life has been a great lesson for me. I knew then, and am sure now, that the temperament I have today came from the experience I got along the way.

◊ *Bridesmaids* premiered in Los Angeles on this day in 2011.

29 APRIL

"Falling out of love is like losing weight. It's a lot easier putting it on than taking it off."

—Aretha Franklin

Breakups and weight loss are two of the most difficult emotional journeys we take in life. As I write, I've had two breakups that broke my heart, my first love and one years later. I'm no shrink, but I learned from those breakups that the key to moving past them was time. I also learned from watching years of *The Oprah Winfrey Show* that the key to losing weight is actually wanting to do it and having a plan. I'm sure there's a lot more to both, but this is a quote book, and I'm trying to be punchy, people!

◇ On April 29, 1967, Aretha Franklin released her iconic song, "Respect."

APRIL

"My point is that, by the time I was your age,
I really thought I knew who I was but I had no
idea. Like for example, when I was your age, I
was dating men. So what I'm saying is, when
you're older, most of you will be gay."
—Ellen DeGeneres

A hilarious way of saying that just because school ends, you're never done learning.

◊ The coming-out episode (aka "The Puppy Episode") of the sitcom *Ellen* aired on April 30, 1997.

"The older you get, the more you realize it's not what happened, it's how you deal with it."

—Tina Turner

Given her life, this sentiment from Tina Turner is as true as her legs are iconic. The image of her crossing that highway in Dallas, finally escaping Ike Turner after another vile attack, is the event that could define Tina Turner, but it's not. How we all face adversity, and where we put it in our lives, will determine who we ultimately become.

◊ Tina Turner's first and only No. 1 on the *Billboard* Hot 100, "What's Love Got to Do With It," was released on May 1, 1984.

2

MAY

"Don't be afraid, and advocate for yourself."

—Kelly Ripa

This is the advice Kelly said she'd give to her younger self. Worth noting that Kelly has given me great advice throughout my career in front of the camera; the best thing she ever told me about hosting my own show was to remember that it's never as good or as bad as you think it is. I've remembered this countless times as I've walked out of my studio thinking I'm either going to win an Emmy for the brilliance that just transpired, or be immediately canceled for my foolishness.

◊ Kelly's sitcom *Hope & Faith* aired its final episode on this day in 2006.

"A rhinestone shines just as good
as a diamond."

—Dolly Parton

This is such a Dolly quote, isn't it? And it's just as pure and real a sentiment as Dolly herself. In the front lines of the *Real Housewives*, I've come in contact with a lot of jewelry, both real and fake. And I'm here to tell you that 99 percent of people cannot tell the difference between a rhinestone and a diamond. I think Dolly's also saying you don't need to be rich/fancy/educated to shine brightly, too. She's right!

◊ On May 3, 1986, Silver Dollar City Tennessee reopened as Dollywood.

MAY

"I've never taken a selfie and I don't plan
to start now."
—Anna Wintour

I salute Ms. Wintour for drawing a line in the sand. In honor of that, here are lifestyle choices that I don't plan to make: get a tattoo, go on TikTok, start social media accounts for my son, go on Keto, partake in SantaCon, and trade in cryptocurrency.

◊ The Met Ball is traditionally held on the first Monday in May, and Wintour famously banned selfies from the event!

5
MAY

"A woman who doesn't wear perfume
has no future."

—Coco Chanel

While this seems like a bit of an exaggeration, I really appreciate a
broad, sweeping statement. We all need to smell pretty!

◊ Coco Chanel debuted her iconic perfume, Chanel No. 5, in her boutique on the rue
Cambon in Paris on this day in 1921.

"True confidence cannot be threatened. When you know that you're great, there's no need to hate."

—Jackée Harry

I love Jackée, her confidence, and another line she made famous: "MAAAAAAAAAAARYYYY!" Her drunken *227* reunion with Regina King is perhaps the most infamous episode of *WWHL*! Fun fact: When I saw how drunk they both were, I thought this show was a train wreck in a bad way, but when my executive producer told me during a commercial break that we were trending worldwide on Twitter, I embraced the mess!

◊ The series finale of *227*, which starred Jackée Harry and Regina King, aired on May 6, 1990.

MAY

"Being a teacher is not what I do, it's who I am."
—Jill Biden

Teachers and nurses are at the top of my list of people who fill my heart up. I'm in awe of the patience, warmth, and sense of service both jobs require. It makes perfect sense that once you're a teacher, that would be the way to define everything else for the rest of your life.

◊ Happy Teacher Appreciation Week!

8

MAY

"When I first moved to New York, someone who thought they knew more than I did said: 'You have to always look like you know where you're going when you get out of the subway.'"

—Maya Rudolph

I'm amused thinking back to 1990, when I was fresh off the bus walking New York City with my eyes in the sky. I hadn't a clue where I was going, but I knew I was in the right place and never wanted to leave.

◊ Book a trip to New York City today!

"If you don't have a Black friend,
you're the problem."
—Wanda Sykes

This speaks for itself.

◊ Wanda Sykes became the first African American woman and first openly LGBTQ
person to host the White House Correspondents' Dinner on May 9, 2009.

"You don't need big boobs to be feminine.
Look at Liberace!"

—Joan Rivers

J oan has a point. Liberace was more feminine than most female gym teachers I've come across, but I'm willing to wager he wore a C cup. They were bigger than they looked!

◊ Joan Rivers won *The Celebrity Apprentice* on this day in 2009.

MAY 11

"I think the men that embrace their female side are the stronger men."

—Grace Jones

One of the revolutions I've seen with the passage of time in my life is that men actually are being given license by society to come closer to embracing their female sides than ever before. Progress!

◊ Grace Jones's fifth studio album, *Nightclubbing*, was released on May 11, 1981.

"Teresa, when we die the viewers will not
be at our funeral."

—Caroline Manzo

What a prescient moment from the season 4 reunion of *The Real Housewives of New Jersey*. I empathize with the Housewives because there's no guidebook about how to handle becoming instantly famous; I often tell them not to lose themselves in all that comes with being on the show. This was Caroline's warning to Teresa that she was losing sight of who she really was in sacrifice to becoming a TV star.

◊ *The Real Housewives of New Jersey* premiered on May 12, 2009.

13 MAY

"The key to beauty is always to be looking at someone who loves you, really."

—Julia Roberts

Makeup, self-tanner, and a fresh haircut can make you feel great, but they don't beat that feeling you get when someone who loves you looks at you. I have to assume JR has had her fair share of loving eyes gazing her way.

◊ *Notting Hill* was released on this day in 1999.

14

MAY

"Don't ever underestimate the power of mentoring someone, or helping some young actor, doing a favor for them, or introducing— everyone needs somebody to help them along when they're first starting out."

—Allison Janney

This is beyond true in every industry. I'm still in touch with my mentors from my internship at *CBS News* in 1988! (There were no cell phones then!) Our lives are about connections we make along the way, and I'm proud to have continued the mentorship vibes for others throughout my own career.

◊ The series finale of *The West Wing* aired on NBC on May 14, 2006.

MAY 15

"I don't know her."

—Mariah Carey

Mariah was responding to a question about JLo on a German TV show and shut the interviewer down with four words that echo through the hallowed halls of the Museum of Legendary Shade! (Why does that place not exist yet, by the way?) I've spoken to Ms. Carey about the quote, which I view as a brilliant put-down, and conversation ender. She has maintained that she meant it literally; of course she knows who JLo is, but she does not know her. Mariah is as great a songwriter (one of the best) as she is a talk-show guest—always "festive" (her word) and forever slaying me with her wit. I'd encourage anybody to give "I don't know her" a whirl.

◊ Mariah Carey released her debut single, "Vision of Love," on May 15, 1990.

"There was a three-year chunk as a teen
where I should have been tranquilized and put
in a cage."
—Melissa McCarthy

The fact that Melissa McCarthy went through a goth phase in high school and turned into such a lovely person should give hope to anyone raising high school barbarians!

◊ The series finale of *Mike & Molly* aired on CBS on this day in 2016.

"Girls have got balls.
They're just a little higher up, that's all."

—Joan Jett

Girls have bigger (metaphorical) balls than most guys I know.

◊ Joan Jett's self-titled debut solo studio album was released on May 17, 1980.

MAY 18

"In the past 15 years . . . I have put on 30 pounds. I live to eat. None of this 'eat to live' stuff for me. I am a champion eater. No carb is safe—no fat, either."

—Candice Bergen

Living to eat is a lifestyle we should all consider.

° *Murphy Brown* ended after ten seasons on CBS on May 18, 1998.

138   ANDY COHEN

"I honestly love my age. I love it. I look forward
to next year . . . as long as I can still wear my
high heels and my short skirts."
—Suzanne Somers

Suzanne always shows up in heels and a mini, and now I know why. I might add that I also *want* Suzanne Somers showing up in heels and a mini. It's the Suzanne we deserve. Side note: I wanna wear my high heels and short skirts when I'm in my seventies, too!

° Suzanne Somers played Chrissy Snow, her breakout role in *Three's Company*, for five years.

MAY

"I'm not a cookie cutter. I cut the cookies,
and I'll cut you."

—Tyra Banks

Well, I guess now we know what Tyra's *Housewives* tagline would be!

◊ *America's Next Top Model* premiered on UPN on May 20, 2003.

21
MAY

"I wasn't meant to get this award before tonight because if I had I wouldn't have that collection of poems and letters and drawings and chocolate cakes you made me to make me feel better."

—Susan Lucci

Lucci's Emmy acceptance speech from 1999—after losing the award NINETEEN consecutive times(!)—is one of the greatest awards moments in history: super-dramatic, performative, diva-esque, emotional, and weepy. It crescendos when she thanks her kids and recalls their comforting gestures over the years. Give this woman an Emmy for that speech!

◊ Susan Lucci finally won her Daytime Emmy on this day in 1999!

22
MAY

"I want minimum information given with
maximum politeness."
—Jackie Kennedy Onassis

This was an instruction to her press secretary, Pamela Turnure. Saying less is sometimes the ultimate power.

◊ Jackie Kennedy became the only First Lady to win an Emmy when she won a special Academy of Television Arts & Sciences Trustees Award, for her famous televised tour of the White House, on this day in 1962. Lady Bird Johnson accepted it on her behalf.

MAY 23

"You never have sex the way people do in the movies. You don't do it on the floor, you don't do it standing up, you don't always have all your clothes off, you don't happen to have on all the sexy lingerie. You know, if anybody ever ripped my clothes, I'd kill them."

—Julianne Moore

I'm not into damaging my clothes, but I otherwise aspire to the rest of this list. Don't you?

◊ *The Lost World: Jurassic Park* was released in the United States on May 23, 1997.

MAY 24

"I was the first one to ever say 'bitch' on television and the censors let me do it because they said, 'Well, it was a nice sweet old lady saying it.'"

—Gilda Radner

Radner is speaking here of her beloved character Emily Litella, but I'd like to think the censors would've let her say the word out of character as well, because she seemed like the sweetest.

◊ Gilda Radner's final episode as a regular on *Saturday Night Live* was May 24, 1980.

"Please stop debating about whether or not
I aged well. Unfortunately, it hurts all three of my
feelings. My body hasn't aged as well as
I have. Blow us."

—Carrie Fisher

This is bursting with humor and truth. That being said, debating whether people have aged well can be fun.

◊ *Star Wars* was released in the United States on May 25, 1977.

MAY

"I like to send John nudes and say
'sorry wrong person.'"

—Chrissy Teigen

Talk about a way to keep things spicy in your marriage! On the one hand, he'll love to see the nude, on the other hand you'll freak him out so much that he'll think you're having an affair and either hate you or find you more desirable. No matter how on the edge it is, find the thing that keeps your relationship spicy.

◊ John Legend's single "All of Me," which is dedicated to Chrissy, became his first No. 1 on the *Billboard* Hot 100 on May 26, 2014.

27 MAY

"At eleven, paying more at the grocer but getting less. We'll tell you how to get the most . . . What the fuck are you doing?"

—Sue Simmons

Legendary New York anchor Sue Simmons getting caught yelling at a PA during a live promo was a haunting and hilarious reminder to be careful when miked! Sue further solidified her place in TV news history with this one. Watch it on YouTube because there's real fire in her delivery!

◊ Happy birthday, Sue Simmons!

"A blow job is the window to the soul."
—Bethenny Frankel

I'm not sure what this means, but I love this line and always enjoy how Bethenny spoke things into facts.

◊ The series finale of *Bethenny Ever After* aired on Bravo on this day in 2012.

"I'm much happier on my own. I can spend as much time with somebody as I want to spend, but I'm not looking to be with somebody forever or live with someone. I don't want somebody in my house."

—Whoopi Goldberg

Whoopi doesn't want somebody in her house, and I believe it and share her sentiment! Puttering around my house alone after Ben goes to bed is one of my favorite activities, and one that I truly mastered during our endless quarantine. Add a dog and you're never *really* alone, but you get to do exactly what you want.

◊ *Sister Act* was released on May 29, 1992.

MAY

"My biggest critics are the people who've never read me. It doesn't bother me at all."
—Jackie Collins

I loved Jackie Collins's insanely dishy books growing up, and I got to know her years later because she was a huge *Housewives* fan. (Side note: I loved how she pronounced the name Teresa.) And I relate to her sentiment because usually my or the *Housewives'* biggest critics are people who don't actually watch the show. The simple idea of it all is just abhorrent to them, which is just fine, but I don't want to particularly hear about it.

◊ Start a Jackie Collins book today; you won't be able to put it down!

31 MAY

"Maybe what a gay icon is, is a person who is rooted for—in other words, cheered on— by people who feel different."

—Liza Minnelli

It takes one to know one, Liza! If you want to see why we love Liza, go to YouTube and type in:"Liza Minnelli New York New York Live Best Performance of this Song."You're welcome!

◇ The concert film *Liza with a "Z"* was shot on this day in 1972, at the Lyceum Theatre in New York.

"If no one can behave themselves, then you'll all
go home. I give you permission. All go home
because I decorated! I cooked! I made it nice!"

—Dorinda Medley

This quote comes at the tail end of a masterful soliloquy by Dorinda
Medley in season 8 of *The Real Housewives of New York City*. She'd
worked hard to prepare her home in the Berkshires to host her friends,
who behaved poorly. It struck a chord with millions of people, and I was
reminded of similar moments in my home on special occasions when
my mom had been working her ass off and would lose her mind right
before the guests came at the slightest indiscretion of my father. She
would put on a hostess face when the guests arrived, but her meltdowns
stayed with me for the rest of the night.

◊ Dorinda Medley had this epic meltdown in season 8, episode 9 of *RHONY*, "December:
Berkshires County," that aired on this day in 2016.

JUNE

"I have to be seen to be believed."
—Queen Elizabeth II

This seems like such an oddly fierce thing to come from the mouth of the pint-sized monarch with the square purse, so we have to celebrate it.

◊ Elizabeth was crowned Queen of England on June 2, 1953. Also, happy birthday to ME!

3

JUNE

"I'm always in love. If it's not with a man,
it's something else. I love beauty. I love the sky I
see outside the window. There's so much beauty
in the world."
—Gloria Vanderbilt

Gloria Vanderbilt remained optimistic until the end of her life, always convinced that a great love or adventure was around the next corner. I like to look at her beautiful new grandson and think she sent him to remind us all of her spirit.

◊ Happy birthday, Anderson Cooper!

4
JUNE

"If you tell the truth, you don't have to remember what you said."
—Emily Rosenfeld

My sister is right! Sometimes it's tough to come out with the truth, but it's almost always followed by a sense of relief.

◊ The truth is that today is National Donut Day!

JUNE

"The only rule is don't be boring and dress cute wherever you go. Life is too short to blend in."
—Paris Hilton

Dress cute, kids! And carry a small dog! This is the perfect Paris life mantra, but it applies to all of us. Dress cute!

◊ Paris Hilton's song "Stars Are Blind" was released on this day in 2006.

6

JUNE

"And New York City, who told the greatest story
of all the last few years."
—Sarah Jessica Parker

Of course SJ thanked New York City in her Emmy acceptance speech after a *Sex and the City* win! One of the gifts of being friends with Parker is that she consistently appreciates and calls out often overlooked points of beauty of the city we love—an impeccably organized bodega, a secret city garden behind a chain-link fence, sidewalk graffiti bursting with color. Look around. Appreciate the small wonders.

◊ *Sex and the City* premiered on HBO on June 6, 1998.

7

JUNE

"When you're trying to soar, you can't have folks holding you down. Find a way if not to cut ties, then at least to loosen them a bit."

—Bevy Smith

It takes strength and clarity to have an awareness of people negatively impacting you and to redefine those friendships. Taking control and recalibrating the roles people play in your life is an essential part of growth. (Do I sound like Iyanla? Good—that's what I was going for!)

◊ Today is a great day to get rid of someone in your life who's bringing you down!

8

JUNE

"I cannot stress enough that the answer to a lot of your life's questions is often in someone else's face. Try putting your iPhones down every once in a while and look at people's faces. People's faces will tell you amazing things. Like if they are angry or nauseous, or asleep."

—Amy Poehler

This was Poehler's advice to the Harvard graduating class of 2011, and it's even more prescient today. I'm hoping the next generation turns against their phones, but I hold out little hope.

◊ Let's all try to limit our phone use today and see how it feels!

JUNE 9

"If sex is such a natural phenomenon, how come there are so many books on how to do it?"

—Bette Midler

Good point, but I think the reason is that sex sells. The better question is who is actually reading the books about how to do it?

◊ Happy National Sex Day! The unofficial holiday is celebrated every year on June 9 because 6/9 resembles a certain sexual position . . .

"When I was a little kid we'd have to go to bed
after *I Dream of Jeannie*. I didn't know it was
7:30, but I knew when *I Dream of Jeannie* was
over we were in trouble. I was like six, so I used
to turn the volume down because I didn't yet
know about clocks . . ."

—Rosie O'Donnell

My entire childhood experience was timed by what came on television. After school was always *The Brady Bunch*, after dinner we'd ride
the ABC lineup, and it was lights out at ten. The weekend mornings
could not come early enough, and I'd be in front of the TV before the
cartoons.

◊ *The Rosie O'Donnell Show* premiered on June 10, 1996.

JUNE 11

"The nice thing, in the morning I wake up and I'm all by myself and I'm happy and I don't have anybody in the bed that's gonna fart . . ."

—Debbie Reynolds

This is a great way to feel better about sleeping alone. Is there anything more unpleasant than a fart that's not your own, stinking up your bed??? Side note: I can't believe farts were on Debbie's radar.

◊ *The Unsinkable Molly Brown* was released theatrically on June 11, 1964.

JUNE 12

"All I see in the mirror every morning is a face
that needs washing."

—Elizabeth Taylor

And all I see in the morning are teeth that need brushing! Oh Liz,
marry me!

◊ *Cleopatra* was released in the United States on June 12, 1963.

"I would have been perfect as a man."

—Annie Lennox

And I feel like I would've been a decent woman, but for the life of me I can't decide how I'd dress. I think I'd either want to be in sequin jumpsuits or muumuus or beach coverups, but none of these options seem practical, and I have little hope I'd be able to carry off the jumpsuit. The muumuu, on the other hand, is within my skill set. The more I think about it, I might be a terrible woman.

◊ The Eurythmics' hit song "There Must Be an Angel (Playing with My Heart)" was released on this day in 1985.

JUNE 14

"Don't try to teach a pig to sing.
It doesn't work, and it annoys the pig."

—Judy Sheindlin

That's so Judy to call men pigs. By the way, would you or would you not watch a sitcom called "That's So Judy!"? I think I just struck gold.

◊ On June 14, 2013, *Judge Judy* won its first Daytime Emmy for Outstanding Legal/Courtroom Program, after its fifteenth nomination.

15 JUNE

"I'm like Johnny Cash. I only wear black."

—Adele

So Sonja Morgan's neutral is leopard, and Adele's is black—the point is to find yours and stick with it! (I'd say black is probably universally more versatile.)

◊ On June 15, 2013, Adele was awarded an MBE (Member of the Most Excellent Order of the British Empire) in the Queen's Birthday Honours list for services to music.

JUNE

"I'm very conscious of my limitations, so I didn't want to tackle it and make a fool of myself. So I wanted to check it out first."

—Olivia Newton-John

Olivia Newton-John was so nervous about doing *Grease*—even though John Travolta knew she was meant for the part—that she wouldn't agree to the role until they did a screen test. Considering what a classic performance in a landmark movie that is, it's mind-boggling but completely humanizing to think she could've had self-doubts. I guess we all do.

◊ *Grease* was released in the United States on June 16, 1978.

JUNE 17

"I wish I had invented sex."
—Debbie Harry

The printing press. The car. The computer. But what came before all revolutions? Sex! Thank you, Debbie Harry, for making me realize that I've been taking for granted the greatest invention of them all. Sex is more brilliant than any new iPhone that Apple is going to force you to buy in six months. I, too, wish I had invented sex and got a patent for it because then I would be the richest man in the world without having to steal your data or crush small businesses with my online retail store.

◊ Blondie's first single, "X Offender," was released on June 17, 1976.

18

JUNE

"Peanut butter is the greatest invention
since Christianity."

—Dianna Vreeland

I think Vreeland and Debbie Harry should've fought this one out. As a referee for the people, I'm gonna give this round to Debbie. I'll take sex over peanut butter any day, wouldn't you?

◊ On this day in 1858, Charles Darwin decided to publish his theory of evolution, which is also certainly a better invention than peanut butter.

JUNE

"I have no interest in an inferior martini."

—Patricia Altschul

I wish I loved martinis because they're so damn sexy, chic, and classy. I don't. Does that make me ugly, unfashionable, and low-rent? Um, I gotta go . . .

◇ June 19 is National Martini Day in the United States!

"You don't transcribe? You do now!"

—Erin Moriarty

This was in response to the *CBS News* correspondent's sassy intern who, when asked to transcribe an interview, mouthed off to his superior that he "didn't transcribe." Yes, I was that sassy kid, and from that moment on, I learned not only how to transcribe but to watch my mouth! Thanks for the lesson, Erin!

◊ The first day of my fateful internship at *CBS News* was June 20, 1988.

21 JUNE

"You can call me burnt toast, Oompa Loompa,
orange freak as long as I know that I'm tan.
Call me whatever you want."

—Snooki

For most of my life, I shared Snooki's love of being tan. I considered tanning one of my favorite pastimes (a hobby even!), thought I looked and felt better when tan, and felt the state of being tan somehow elevated me. In 2016, that all came crashing down when I (inevitably) discovered melanoma and was told I could never satisfy my tanorexia again. I adapted just in time; dads don't have time to lie out in the sun anyway!

◊ *Snooki & J Woww* premiered on MTV on this day in 2012.

"Pain is a teacher."

—Joni Mitchell

I'm not Oprah, or Joni, but I firmly believe that if we can all walk away with some bit of growth from our own struggles, then we are growing as humans.

◇ Joni Mitchell's fourth studio album, *Blue*, was released on June 22, 1971.

JUNE

"Were you silent, or were you silenced?"
—Oprah Winfrey

This iconic question is extremely versatile in everyday conversation. Throw it in and watch your friends' faces fill with delight!

◇ *Suits*, which starred Meghan Markle for seven seasons, premiered on USA on June 23, 2011.

JUNE

"Would you like a sandwich, Andrew?"
—Connie Chung

When I was a desk assistant at *CBS News*, I was sent to drop off some research for Connie Chung. Little did I know that meant leaving the packages with her doorman. When I showed up at her front door, she wasn't mad but instead offered me a sandwich. Do you think I ever forgot her kindness? NO! Did I have the good sense not to accept the sandwich? YES!

◊ CNN's *Connie Chung Tonight* launched on this date in 2002 and lasted less than a year.

JUNE

"I don't think of all the misery,
but of the beauty that still remains."
—Anne Frank

Thank you, Anne Frank.

◇ Anne Frank's book, known then as *The Secret Annex,* was published in the Netherlands on this day in 1947.

176   ANDY COHEN

26

JUNE

"You don't have to be age 20 and size zero to
be sexually viable or viable as a woman."
—Belinda Carlisle

I'm including this quote partly because it's clearly true but mainly because Belinda Carlisle has kicked ass from before any of us heard the first note of *Beauty and the Beat*. I'm a huge Go-Go's fan and love how confident they all were musically and sexually; they behaved with no apologies, like an all-male punk band would. The Rolling Stones are collectively 756 years old, and they're considered just as sexy as they were 900 years ago, which is why I also fully condone Madonna showing us her ass until she chooses otherwise.

◊ "Vacation"by the Go-Go's was released on this day in 1982. The song was the lead single from their second album.

27

JUNE

"Letting your freak flag fly is something,
no matter who you are, that takes great bravery,
straight up."

—Sarah Silverman

Sarah said this in an interview with a gay magazine, so she was speaking directly to that community, but this applies to everybody. Let it fly.

◊ Happy Gay Pride!

28

JUNE

"Well, even Louis Vuitton makes mistakes."
—Countess Luann

Just because it's designer, doesn't mean it's any good. I could've saved a lot of wasted money at the cash register of Fred Segal if I'd remembered the countess tossing this lob at Alex McCord in season 4. Side note: When I first saw Lu deliver this line, I was dead, and she went up many notches in my esteem.

◇ Luann's second single, "Chic C'est la Vie," was released on this day in 2011.

"Instead of penetrating, I think [men] all need to be penetrated once. Then they'll understand what it's like to receive instead of give."
—Grace Jones

I once was at an Oscar party packed with every famous person you've ever seen. I found myself in a conversation with Madonna and at one point asked her what percentage of men at the party she thought would enjoy a finger up their butt. "One hundred percent," she responded.

◊ Grace Jones's first role in a major studio film was *Conan the Destroyer*, which was released in the United States on June 29, 1984.

"In my long career [I've] played so many
extraordinary women that basically I am getting
mistaken for one."

—Meryl Streep

I love how humble she always is, and I will use her humble moment to brag about the time she paid me a compliment: I once found myself at a charades party with Streep (don't ask). I was unprepared (drunk) to perform in front of her and was bombing the clue (no memory of what it was) very badly. Streep, from the back of the room, announced, "I don't know what he's doing, but I never want him to stop!"

◊ Today might be Meryl's lucky day: both *Mamma Mia* and *The Devil Wears Prada* premiered today (in 2008 and 2006).

1

JULY

"Please don't make me a joke. End the interview with what I believe. I don't mind making jokes, but I don't want to look like one . . . I want to be an artist, an actress with integrity . . . If fame goes by, so long, I've had you, fame. If it goes by, I've always known it was fickle. So at least it's something I experienced, but that's not where I live."

—Marilyn Monroe

This heartbreaking quote is from Marilyn's last taped interview, with Richard Meryman, published in *Life* magazine a few days before her death in 1962. It sticks in my throat that she's pleading with the interviewer to regard her as more than her image, and reading her words makes me revere and respect her.

◊ The film *Gentlemen Prefer Blondes* made its world premiere in Atlantic City on this day in 1953.

2
JULY

"You know, my grandma lived to be 110, and she drank alcohol, like, every day. I don't drink every day. But if somebody's like, 'Shots!' I'm like, 'Yes!' If someone says, 'Bacon!' I'm like, 'Yes!' She lived. I definitely live."

—Gabrielle Union

BRB—I'm off to get shots with a bacon chaser.

◊ *Being Mary Jane* premiered on BET on July 2, 2013.

3

JULY

"Nothing tastes as good as skinny feels."

—Kate Moss

Moss has since publicly said she regrets this now-iconic quote, but I still love the sentiment. Yes, we should feel good at every size, and yes, diversity is fantastic. But that doesn't take away that it feels great to fit into our smallest jeans, as long as we're staying healthy. When I got COVID, I was down to my high school weight, and I can honestly say that my weight loss and binging *Game of Thrones* were the only good things about those few weeks.

◊ Kate Moss's second magazine cover was for the July 1990 issue of the magazine *The Face*. She was only sixteen years old.

4
JULY

"Complacency is not something we have the right to live in no more. The tears that I cry at night, the tears I know you all cry at night, wipe them in the morning and do something about it."
—Porsha Williams

I'm amazed and impressed by Porsha Williams's journey in life. We met her as a stifled wife confused by the Underground Railroad, and she was propelled into a world of activism. She's used her platform for good while not losing sight of remaining entertaining as hell!

◊ Happy Independence Day!

JULY 5

"Cancer isn't at all funny, but a big part of
dealing with it has been finding the funny
moments. The old cliché about laughter being
the best medicine turns out to be true . . ."

—Julia Louis-Dreyfus

Pretty much no one has made us laugh as much as Julia Louis-Dreyfus, and she even made her fight with cancer funny (and empowering). Laughter is the key to happiness, and I'm often blown away by the amount of people I hear from facing terminal illness who tell me that the *Housewives* is their great escape. When things are bad, it's important to picture Luann falling in a bush and give yourself a giggle . . .

◊ *Seinfeld* premiered on NBC on July 5, 1989.

JULY

"I, somewhere inside, knew and sort of wanted
to go to jail . . . just to find some peace."
—Lindsay Lohan

Lohan confessed this to Oprah in 2013, and it's a lesson that if you're ever in a place where you need to go to jail to get some peace, take a hard look at yourself. Our lives may not be as dramatic as Lindsay's (hopefully), but if you ever feel like you might be self-sabotaging, scared of your potential, don't be!

◊ On this day in 2010, Lindsay Lohan was sentenced to ninety days in jail for failing to attend her court-ordered weekly alcohol education classes.

7

JULY

"Wakin' up in the morning, thinking about so many things, I just wish things would get better, I'm trying to get rid of them, but nothing seems to stay the same."

—Gia Guidice

You never know what'll resurface from your past and resonate with millions of people on TikTok. I certainly never could've imagined that this song (which was originally a sad statement about the disarray in her family) would have a first life, much less an even bigger second one! When you look back on it now, though, it lands!

◊ Also in pop music history, Bruce Springsteen's *Born in the USA* started a four-week run at #1 on the charts on this day in 1984.

JULY

8

"I really think a champion is defined not by their wins but by how they can recover when they fall."

—Serena Williams

Not to compare Williams to Lisa Rinna, but look how many House-wives have had truly horrible seasons and come back on top the following year! Sometimes champions are reborn!

◇ The Women's Tennis Association ranked Serena Williams No. 1 in singles for the first time on this day in 2002.

JULY

"Don't waste your time feeling old
when you're young."
—Savannah Guthrie

I've included this sentiment said a few different ways because it comes up so much in life, and it's a good reminder.

◊ Savannah Guthrie's first episode as co-anchor of *Today* aired on July 9, 2012.

JULY

10

"The truth will set you free,
but first it will piss you off!"

—Gloria Steinem

I could've chosen Steinem's quote calling the *Housewives* a "female minstrel show," but I decided to go with one I agreed with!

◊ Gloria Steinem delivered her Address to the Women of America at the opening conference of the National Women's Political Caucus on July 10, 1971.

11
JULY

"Disobedience is my joy!"

—Princess Margaret

My entire base of knowledge of Princess Margaret comes from *The Crown*, but this quote tracks with everything I love about her. She had a devilish energy that always seemed to make things more exciting. Call her a civil disobedient!

◊ Princess Margaret's divorce from Antony Armstrong-Jones was finalized on July 11, 1978. It was the first divorce of a senior member of the British royal family since 1901.

JULY

"Don't be thirsty and hold in every single fart
when you're around that person . . . I have
engaged my core so much around Miche,
it's wild."

—Phoebe Robinson

I appreciate Robinson's perspective about befriending famous people
like Michelle Obama, but I'd argue in favor of holding in your farts! If I
farted in front of a FLOTUS, I'd never let myself live it down. (I farted
in front of Celine Dion once, and I think of it every time one of her
songs comes on, which is more than you might think.) Hold it in!

◊ Robinson's podcast, *Sooo Many White Guys*, debuted on this day in 2016.

JULY

"I have my undergarments that are too tight on,
so I forget the story."

—Jennifer Coolidge

Coolidge is one of a kind and used this brilliant excuse when she lost her way during a 2020 *WWHL* appearance. When someone is this honest, all you can do is laugh and forgive.

◊ *Legally Blonde* was released on July 13, 2001.

14

JULY

"Okay, what do you think about Dula Peep?"
—Wendy Williams

Only Wendy Williams can get away with continually butchering names (here: Dua Lipa) on national television. I do it, and I'm mortified until the next show; I don't think Wendy thinks twice about it, and I celebrate her confidence.

JULY

"Blond is a way of life. You face the world like
an Amazon. I survived the catastrophes
in my life because of the strength that my blonde
hair gives me."

—Donatella Versace

I think this is kind of ridiculous, but it's perfectly Donatella. No
catastrophe is a match for blonde ambition, and wherever you can find
confidence, go for it! Side note: Was her hair ever naturally blond?

◊ Gianni Versace was murdered on this day in 1997. After his death, Donatella took over
the Versace brand and held her first haute couture show a year later.

JULY

"I knew I wasn't gonna be the girl who got in
this play, so I would make the play. And I knew
I wouldn't be the girl who maybe hung out with
this crowd, so we created like a crazy freaky
drama crowd. I look back and I am so grateful
for the opportunities I did not have."

—Kathy Najimy

How's that for making it happen for yourself? Tell your sons and
daughters to be like Najimy!

◊ *Hocus Pocus* was released in the United States on July 16, 1993.

JULY

"I'm probably like 160 pounds right now and can catch a dick whenever I want."

—Amy Schumer

Well, isn't this inspiring to gals of all sizes!

◊ *Trainwreck*, a film Amy Schumer wrote and starred in, was released in the United States on July 17, 2015.

JULY

"Kim, would you stop taking pictures of yourself?
Your sister's going to jail."

—Kris Jenner

There is a time and a place to take selfies, people! Kris Jenner famously said this to Kim Kardashian in season 3 of *KUWTK* when Khloe violated her probation after her DUI arrest, and it instantly became iconic. Listen to your mothers, kids . . .

◊ On July 18, 2008, Khloe Kardashian reported to jail to serve time for violation of probation.

JULY

"When someone is cruel or acts like a bully, you don't stoop to their level. No, our motto is, when they go low, we go high."

—Michelle Obama

How am I gonna put out a book of quotes from women I love and leave this one out? No-brainer.

◇ Michelle Obama launched her When We All Vote initiative on July 19, 2018, to encourage young people to vote.

JULY

"I pooed in his shoes . . . Because he was
putting me through a lot of dookie so I decided
he needed to walk in it."
—Tiffany Haddish

Of course, I know I just sang the praises of Michelle Obama's creed of "going high," but sometimes you may need to go low to get your point across! This is not really about revenge but more about making someone who wronged you really understand your pain. Tiffany's logic is sound; when a selfish, faithless partner puts you through a lot of metaphorical shit, perhaps they should literally have to walk in that shit. Then, they'll see how much you suffered and may think twice before cheating again!

◊ On this day in 2020, Haddish showed off her newly shaved head on Instagram, saying that when water hit her head it felt like kisses from God!

JULY

"It took me a lifetime to get here . . . I'm not going anywhere."

—Diana Ross

This is one of the greatest moments in concert history, and I need to properly set the scene here: It's 1983 and Diana Ross is onstage in the driving rain in front of hundreds of thousands of people in Central Park, as the wind blows her mane of hair perfectly behind her. The NYPD want her to cancel the show so that everyone can leave safely, but this queen diva—in the midst of singing "Ain't No Mountain High Enough"—triumphantly declares to her audience that she'll never leave them. They belong to her, and she belongs to them. And indeed she had been waiting a lifetime to get there, all the way from the projects of Detroit. She continued singing in the driving rain for about forty-five minutes and rescheduled for the next sunny day. But that line for me encompasses true love between a superstar and her audience.

◊ On this day in 1983, Diana Ross's iconic Central Park performance (to raise funds for a children's park) was cut short because of a lightning storm. She performed the show again the next day.

JULY

"Is there a de-asshole superpower?
I would de-asshole some people."

—Kristen Johnston

This was K-Jo's response when asked what her superpower would be, and that's a Marvel movie I'd pay to see on opening day!

◊ *Captain America* was released on July 22, 2011.

JULY

"Only terrorists and a**holes order mojitos.
I can keep my composure on anyone—
that's my job. But in my head I'm saying,
'I hate you so much.'"
—Kate Chastain

I understand how a mojito could annoy any bartender or waitress, but repeating Kate's mantra in your head might be a way to deal with ass-holes.

◊ Today is National Refreshment Day. I would caution against ordering a mojito.

JULY

"I leaked. I'm gonna own it. I'm not going to lie about it. I did it. Just a little bit. Whatever. I don't care. Tell me none of you have ever leaked. Everyone has leaked one time in their life."

—Vicki Gunvalson

Vicki admitting to peeing the bed during a laugh attack is the definition of owning it and not being ashamed. Everybody poops (see Zoila Chavez) and pees!

◊ Today is National Tequila Day! Whoop it up, but keep your legs crossed!

JULY

"When I tell people the way I feel, they hear me, but they're not really listening."

—Britney Spears

This absolutely breaks my heart. Listen.

◊ Britney Spears's song "Lucky" was released on this day in 2000.

26

JULY

"I think marriage is all about timing. Getting married is insanity; I mean, it's a risk—who knows if you're going to be together forever? But you both say, 'We're going to take this chance, in the same spirit.'"

—Cate Blanchett

I think every bride and groom should take a moment to pray on this sentiment on the morning of their wedding day. It certainly takes the pressure off the whole "till death do us part" vibe, which can be a bit ... suffocating, shall we say.

◊ The film *Blue Jasmine* was released in New York and Los Angeles on this day in 2013. Cate Blanchett won the Academy Award for Best Actress the following year.

27

JULY

"Reclaiming my time! Reclaiming my time! Reclaiming my time!"

—Maxine Waters

I'm sorry I have to do this, but let's go back to the first year of the Trump administration when Treasury secretary Steve Mnuchin, the worst John Oliver look-alike there is, testified before the House Financial Services Committee to discuss the state of the international finance system. In the hearing, Representative Maxine Waters questioned Mnuchin about why he had not responded to her letters regarding Trump's financial ties to Russia. As he tried to pivot from the question by complimenting her to run out the clock, Auntie Maxine uttered these words and turned a House procedural rule into a feminist mantra! I hate when people waste my time, and I've often wanted to pull a Maxine. You know what, even if you're not a congresswoman, never be afraid to reclaim your time when someone is wasting it!

◇ Maxine Waters said this on this date in 2017.

JULY

28

"Things didn't go exactly the way I planned, but you know what? I'm doing OK. Here's what helped most of all: remembering who I am, where I come from, and what I believe . . . Long walks in the woods. Organizing my closets. Chardonnay helped a little, too."

—Hillary Clinton

Something I have always admired about Secretary Clinton is her ability to pick herself back up and shake off whatever was thrown at her. We can all agree that the 2016 election was a real doozy, especially for Hillary, so it's no surprise that it took her some extra help to get through that devastating (electoral college) loss. Despite all her accomplishments and accusations of being "robotic," Hillary, like many of us, turned to chardonnay to get through the pain. Now that's relatable!

◊ Hillary Clinton accepted the Democratic Party's nomination for president on this day in 2016. She was the first and so far only woman to be nominated by a major party for president.

29
JULY

"Well, there were three of us in this marriage,
so it was a bit crowded."
—Princess Diana

The more I hear about the crap that Diana had to endure, the more my heart goes out to her. But it's worth pointing out that I've met a few thruples that are doing great. It may not have worked for Diana, Charles, and Camilla, but it works fine for Ben, Mark, and Steve!

◊ Diana married Prince Charles on this day in 1981, with an estimated global TV audience of 750 million people.

JULY

"Who gon' check me, boo?"

—Shereé Whitfield

If this isn't the ultimate clapback, I don't know what is. It works in almost any circumstance and can mean a rainbow of things. The bottom line is that it means "Don't f with me."

◊ Sheree Whitfield uttered this iconic clapback on the season 2 premiere of *The Real Housewives of Atlanta*, which aired on July 30, 2009.

31
JULY

"Your poo poo don't smell?"
—Zoila Chavez

Flipping Out's long-suffering housekeeper Zoila was the one person who could say anything to Jeff Lewis and get away with it, and we all loved her for it. Her reminder that everyone's poop smells is truly the great equalizer between all of us. Keep it in mind when you see someone you envy!

◇ *Flipping Out* premiered on Bravo on July 31, 2007.

"My mom said to me, 'You know, sweetheart, one day you should settle down and marry a rich man.' And I said, 'Mom—I am a rich man.'"

—Cher

You, Cher, are whoever the f you want to be! I do know you're powerful, smart, driven, and in control. And I just love a woman with that kind of confidence and sense of herself. It's a great way to be.

◊ *The Sonny & Cher Comedy Hour* premiered on CBS on August 1, 1971.

AUGUST

"Being funny got me famous, and being famous is almost as bad for dating as being funny."

—Gilda Radner

It kills me that men find funny women too intimidating to date. It also kills me that someone as brilliant as Radner wouldn't have men lining up for her. It warms my heart that she and Gene Wilder ultimately found each other; theirs seemed like real love. Side note: Dating when famous is weird. People know more about you than you do them, and they're often not letting on how much they really do know. It's all very confusing.

◊ Gilda Radner's one-woman show, *Live from New York*, opened on Broadway on August 2, 1979.

3

AUGUST

"You can disagree without being disagreeable."
—Ruth Bader Ginsburg

This is a great mantra for all of us who love our country and get riled up by cable news. We're swirling in divisiveness, and if we could figure out a way to heed RBG's advice, maybe we could start working together.

◊ Ruth Bader Ginsburg was confirmed as an associate justice to the Supreme Court on this day in 1993.

AUGUST

"Things aren't so good that they couldn't
be worse."
—Evelyn Cohen

Thanks for the upper, Mom! Seriously, thanks for always keeping things in perspective even though you're killing my buzz.

◊ On this day in 1970, Jim Morrison was arrested for drunkenness. Many other more horrible things happened on this day in history, like Anne Frank's capture in 1944, proving that things can always be worse.

5
AUGUST

"Some girls are just born with glitter
in their veins."

—Paris Hilton

And those are the girls I'm drawn to! Also, isn't it interesting to find out years later that Paris says she was playing the character of a dumb, glittery blonde all those years. I believe her.

◊ The series finale of *The Simple Life* aired on August 5, 2007, on E!

6
AUGUST

"When you're a hammer, everything's a nail."

—Liza Persky

I'm constantly repeating this line I first heard from my friend Liza. There are certain people in the world who make problems wherever they go—they're HAMMERS. Stay away from them. They're gonna pound you like a nail!

◊ In August of 1966, Peppermint Patty made her debut in the *Peanuts* comic strip. (Peppermint Patty was a hammer!)

7

AUGUST

"I just had to get fucking, that's all. Bitch feels baptized. I came back to fucking life, bitch."

—Cardi B

Two weeks after announcing their split, Cardi and Offset were seen together on vacation. Before people could start rumors that they were back together, Cardi shut it down with an honest explanation; she needed sex! Sometimes when you miss the D so much, you have to call up that ex. As long as you don't get tangled back in drama, go for it!

◊ Cardi B's single "WAP" was released on this day in 2020.

AUGUST

"I always knew that saying the unsayable was going to be a powerful thing."
—Phoebe Waller-Bridge

I love saying the unsayable, to the point that I'm worried I'll be canceled just because I can't resist saying what I'm not supposed to say! So pray for me that I continue pushing the envelope just to the very edge of what I can get away with, and say what you have to say, too.

◊ Phoebe Waller-Bridge first performed the play version of *Fleabag* in August of 2013 at the Edinburgh Festival Fringe.

AUGUST

"What would Beyoncé do,
but let me make it a little ratchet."
—Megan Thee Stallion

While accepting the Grammy for Best Rap Song for "Savage" with Beyoncé in 2021, Megan Thee Stallion explained that she wanted to grow up to be like Beyoncé but with this twist. And it worked! I'm not gonna call her the ratchet Beyoncé, but I love that she called herself that!

◊ Be like Beyoncé today! Or Megan!

AUGUST

"Now I don't like three-ways, I've had a few. I don't enjoy them . . . they make me feel like a competitive eater."

—Margaret Cho

M argaret Cho is hilarious. That's today's lesson.

◊ Consider a three-way, or a buffet, today!

AUGUST

"Show me someone who never gossips,
and I'll show you someone who isn't interested
in people."
—Barbara Walters

Barbara Walters was America's yenta. And I dig anyone who can make me feel better about gossiping.

◊ *The View*, which Barbara Walters co-created and co-hosted, premiered on ABC on this day in 1997.

AUGUST

"It's very hard to hate someone if you look them in the eye and recognize them as a human being."

—Maya Angelou

I remember seeing actors on *All My Children* and deciding I HATED THEM. My vitriol at, say Dixie Chandler, was directed at some whimsy I decided was unworthy of my affection. Years later I went to the studio to interview Susan Lucci (for the full story, see *Most Talkative*!), and stalked, I mean *saw* "Dixie" and others dissolving onto Columbus Avenue as they exited the inauspicious West Sixty-Seventh Street studio. It was then that I recognized them as human beings. And it is now that I recognize that Ms. Angelou might roll her eyes at my base analogy. It works though!

◊ Maya Angelou's first collection of poems, *Just Give Me a Cool Drink of Water 'fore I Diiie*, was released on August 12, 1971.

"La La Land."

—Faye Dunaway

W hat can we learn from Faye Dunaway's epic blunder? Ask for help when confused, no matter how high profile the moment. As a matter of fact, the more high profile, the better to ask because you don't wanna mess it up!

◊ *Bonnie and Clyde* was released in the United States on August 13, 1967.

14
AUGUST

"I'm not overweight. I'm just nine inches
too short."

—Shelley Winters

This is the correct response to any ass that comments on your weight.

◊ *A Place in the Sun* was released in Los Angeles on August 14, 1951.

15 AUGUST

"I say sure get a tattoo, I have a number of them myself. I would say put it somewhere as you age that doesn't sag."

—Susan Sarandon

Sarandon shared this sentiment on *WWHL*, and it was something of an aha moment for me because sagging, aged skin is one of the things that's kept me from getting a tattoo. Barbed wire around a bicep looks hot on someone in their twenties and like dental floss around a withered grape on someone in their sixties. Also, what if something that seemed cool in your twenties (like barbed wire) doesn't resonate in your forties? The whole tattoo thing seems like a total land mine to me. But maybe I just have commitment issues. OK, go on with your day. (Maybe today's the day you get a tattoo!?)

◊ The film *The Rocky Horror Picture Show* was released in London on August 15, 1975.

AUGUST 16

"I think everyone steals from each other.
I think that's the only way that we keep alive as
far as learning."

—Ella Fitzgerald

Like the woman who said it, this quote is just real. We all copy from people or are influenced by people. Successful people take what works from other talented people and make it their own. For example, I got the idea for this book from my friend Hoda Kotb, who published two quote-a-day books! Thanks, Hodes!

◊ Ella Fitzgerald and Louis Armstrong began recording their album *Ella and Louis* on this day in 1956.

17

AUGUST

"I think one manifestation of integrity is holding a grudge. Saying no is a little different. Holding a grudge is the modern equivalent of having standards."

—Fran Lebowitz

Lots of people say that holding on to negativity can be unhealthy, but Lebowitz seems energized by her annoyances at people and things, and it works as a gatekeeper for what she lets into her life. It's counterintuitive, but don't knock it till you've tried it.

◊ Happy birthday Sean Penn, one of America's favorite Grudge Holders!

18
AUGUST

"I'm gonna be like seventy-eight years old in a
bikini on the beach."
—Samantha Bee

Samantha Bee refers to old age as the "fuck it" era of life, and I am
here for it. I'm gonna be in a G-string at seventy-eight.

◊ Today is National Black Cat Appreciation Day, which is as arbitrary as if I told you it
was National Appreciate a Seventy-Eight-Year-Old in a Bikini Day!

AUGUST

"I have an interesting mind, but I want to smell like a slut, to be honest."

—Lady Gaga

Gaga said this while promoting her perfume, and it made me wonder if I'd seek out the fragrance of . . . a slut. Hmmm. Side note: Gaga peed in a trash can backstage at *WWHL*, and my PA turned it into perfume, and the shiny bottle sits on my set to this day. I have to assume it smells worse than "slut."

◊ Lady Gaga's debut studio album, *The Fame,* was released on August 19, 2008.

AUGUST

"The only thing worse than stale brioche
at a party is stale guests."

—Sonja Morgan

I could not agree with TSTSTD (The Straw That Stirs the Drink) more about this party tip! Anderson Cooper claims I cast my parties like House-wives Reunions, and he may be right. I want there to be a little drama (throw in a couple people who don't get along), surprises (I love when an unannounced guest enters the fray and causes a stir), and, of course, folks who are committed to fun.

◊ Sonja Morgan relaunched her fashion line at Century 21 in season 12, episode 19 of *RHONY*. The episode aired on August 20, 2020.

"I'm Tabatha and I'm taking over."
—Tabatha Coffey

There's no greater meaning to this statement. I just loved the shiver I got down my spine when this fierce Australian busted into a beat hair salon and scared the shit out of its owner with these six words.

◇ *Tabatha Takes Over* premiered on Bravo on this day in 2008.

22 AUGUST

"What fresh hell can this be?"
—Dorothy Parker

Satirist Dorothy Parker allegedly said this every time her apartment doorbell rang, and friends said she wasn't trying to be funny. She meant it. It's a brilliantly biting line that works when your phone rings, too!

◊ On August 22, 1992, the ninety-ninth anniversary of Parker's birth, the United States Postal Service issued a twenty-nine-cent U.S. commemorative postage stamp in the Literary Arts series.

"If I were ever to pass you along in life again,
and you were laying there, dying of thirst, I
would not give you a drink of water. I would let
the vultures take you and do whatever they want
with you, with no ill regrets."

—Sue Hawk

This speech, delivered at Tribal Council in the season 1 finale of *Survivor*, was an instant classic. I found out many years later from that season's winner, Richard Hatch, that Hawk made long, boring, rambling speeches at every Tribal Council of that season, but in being cut down by editors, they came off to viewers like poetic clapbacks. It kind of changed my entire perspective of this dramatic speech, but I still love it.

◊ The finale to the first season of *Survivor* aired on this day in 2000.

AUGUST 24

"Bad cocaine makes you feel (terrible). Probably makes you run for the loo because it's laced with laxatives. Pure cocaine gives you a very light, airy, clear, and extremely pleasant feeling. But really, there's no such thing as good cocaine. I don't believe that people should take it recreationally."

—Anjelica Huston

It really is gross, and I can't emphasize it enough. There are no redeeming qualities to this drug.

◊ Anjelica Huston's film *The Witches* was released in the United States on August 24, 1990.

AUGUST 25

"I remember a lot of people, but when I meet people and I'm stoned, I'm not as good with names."

—Miley Cyrus

You and me both, Miley! Actually, I'm not incredible with names when I'm sober either. It's a horrible attribute, and I no doubt am followed by a wake of people in my past who I've pissed off with my horrible name recognition. If I ever meet you, can I just apologize in advance and let you know that it takes me a minute, and I'm sorry?

◊ Miley Cyrus famously twerked during a performance at the VMAs on August 25, 2013.

26 AUGUST

"My first job is being that bitch,
and I ain't never quit."

—Lizzo

We all know that Lizzo took a DNA test and found out that she is 100 percent that bitch, and the truth is that you can be, too. Maybe your 23andMe would say you're only 37 percent "that bitch" right now, but you can choose to be "that bitch" a little more. Like a job, being "that bitch" is a choice and requires a little bit of work, but once you're a full-time employee at That Bitch, Inc., you'll have the confidence to overcome any obstacles and blow a kiss to the haters as you go after your dreams.

◊ Lizzo's 2017 song, "Truth Hurts," hit No. 1 on the *Billboard* Hot 100 on this day in 2019.

27

AUGUST

"Does Mary Poppins have an orgasm? Does she go to the bathroom? I assure you, she does."

—Julie Andrews

She may be "practically perfect in every way," but Mary Poppins has needs just like the rest of us! You didn't really think Mary could come up with all those songs, take care of spoiled English children, and fly through the sky using an umbrella without some sexual pleasure? Even Mary needs to pee after she drinks too much tea or one too many gin and tonics. No matter how perfect Mary or any person seems, we all have the same needs, wants, and desires. So yes, Mary and Bert the chimney sweep did get it on! (And Mary poops!)

◊ The film *Mary Poppins* was released on August 27, 1964.

28
AUGUST

"People respond well to those that are sure of what they want. What people hate most is indecision. Even if I'm completely unsure, I'll pretend I know exactly what I'm talking about and make a decision."

—Anna Wintour

Being decisive is one of the traits of a great leader. It's also incredibly frustrating being around wishy-washy people, whether in the face of a multitude of menu items or behind the wheel of a car.

◊ *The September Issue*, a documentary following Anna Wintour during the creation of *Vogue*'s September 2007 issue, was released on August 28, 2009.

29 AUGUST

"If anybody says their facelift doesn't hurt,
they're lying. It was like I'd spent the night with
an axe murderer."

—Sharon Osbourne

We all need to understand the reality of getting our face chopped open in the name of vanity! Is it worth it?

◊ Show some love to your face today!

"You hang out with trash, and you start
to smell like garbage."
—Caroline Manzo

$\diamond$

Not exactly rocket science, but when Jersey Housewife Caroline Manzo said this about Danielle Staub (I think she said it to explain why she did not want to be around her), it was never more true. Caroline had that way of turning homespun wisdom into commandments to live by.

◇ The first part to Danielle's last reunion as a full-time Housewife (also known as "The One Where Andy Got Pushed") on *The Real Housewives of New Jersey* aired on August 30, 2010.

31

AUGUST

"There can be a hundred people in a room,
and ninety-nine of them don't believe in you,
but all it takes is one, and it just changes your
whole life."

—Lady Gaga

Gaga was poked fun at for repeating this quote in various iterations during her press tour for *A Star Is Born*, but her sentiment is right on! If we're all lucky enough to find that one person who believes in us, there's no telling what we can do! You may be wondering who my person is, and I've had a few along the way in life, but one that sticks out is Lauren Zalaznick, my boss at Bravo, who saw a future in front of the camera for me and afforded me the opportunity to pursue that dream. Find your person!

◊ *A Star Is Born* premiered at the Venice Film Festival on August 31, 2018.

"There could be a hundred people in the room, and ninety-nine say they liked it, I only remember the one person who didn't."

—Madonna

OK—first of all, can we add this quote to the galaxy of Madonna inspirations in Lady Gaga's life? I'm not saying Gaga had actually read this interview in 1989 (see previous quote), but I just love the connection. OK, now I've gotten that off my chest. This quote is quintessential Madonna. She's always aiming for perfection and always wants to hear the one note that might make it better or worse—just let her decide and move on. One of the many reasons Madonna is Madonna.

◊ On this date in 2009, Madonna's Sticky & Sweet Tour made its final stop in Tel Aviv, Israel.

2
SEPTEMBER

"Whatever gets them excited about reading
is good! If you want them to read my books
don't tell them so. Maybe just leave around a
paperback with a new cover and say, 'I'm not
sure you're ready for that.'"

—Judy Blume

I loved Judy Blume, partly because her books were considered dangerous. They also educated generations of adolescents about tough subjects. Side note: "I'm not sure you're ready for that" is a great reverse-psychology technique I plan to use to con my kids into reading books or watching films.

◊ Happy Back-to-School time! Buy your child a Judy Blume book to celebrate!

3

SEPTEMBER

"I love Madonna. She's the one. What do you really say about her? She's the one? The first time I met her, I was just shaking. And I was like, I studied and worshiped you. And I have, I don't even know what to say . . . And she was just like, 'Thank you. And I love you.'"

—Ariana Grande

I sat next to Ariana Grande at a Madonna concert once, and at one point turned to her and said that'll be you when you're her age. I'm not sure I totally understood at that time that what I was saying was entirely true. Ariana Grande is gonna go the distance like Madge.

◇ Ariana Grande's debut studio album, *Yours Truly*, was released on September 3, 2013.

SEPTEMBER

"I worked at Six Flags—I did the singing and dancing, like all those shows. Any option that was available to make money singing, I was like, 'OK.'"

—Kelly Clarkson

Kelly is so damn real, and so is this sentiment. My first job was as a desk assistant at *CBS News*, and I absolutely could not leave the constantly ringing phones at the news desk unless it was covered by a coworker. I loved my job but felt completely trapped by that desk. A year into the job, I got a promotion and a one-way ticket off the desk. I felt liberated! I still walk around with gratitude that I'm not chained to that desk. Never forget where you came from, folks! Those first jobs help define who we are today and make us appreciate how far we've come.

◇ Kelly Clarkson won *American Idol* on this day in 2002.

SEPTEMBER 5

"I succeeded by saying what everyone else
is thinking."
—Joan Rivers

Joan Rivers definitely spoke her mind and had very few fucks to give,
as they say. This is a woman who was telling Helen Keller jokes till the
day she died. I often wonder how Joan would've fared during the height
of cancel culture. I like to think she would've gotten a pass.

◊ Joan's daytime talk show, *The Joan Rivers Show*, premiered on September 5, 1989.

6

SEPTEMBER

"On my darkest days,
I wear my brightest colors."

—Cyndi Lauper

W hile I have no doubt this is true, I can't imagine Cyndi Lauper leaving her house in drab colors, can you? Cyndi in gray? Nope! In my eyes, Cyndi is a walking rainbow, and that's one of the reasons I love her. (She can belt, too.) I love this sentiment though, and for me it's the color yellow that puts an extra spring in m'step. Lean into the light!

◊ Cyndi Lauper's anthem, "Girls Just Want to Have Fun," was released on September 6, 1983.

"If I don't like a bitch, I don't go to their page.
You want to know why? Because people don't
post when they're doing bad."

—Cardi B

Once again Cardi B wins, here with her breakdown of what's really happening on social media. If you don't like a bitch, don't go to their page! It's fake!

◊ Cardi B threw one of her shoes and lunged at Nicki Minaj at the *Harper's Bazaar* ICONS party on this day in 2018.

SEPTEMBER

"We have to make the choice—every single day—to exemplify the truth, the respect, and the grace that we wish for this world."

—Oprah Winfrey

Let me be the millionth person to tell you that Oprah's shit doesn't stink. It actually does, which makes me love her even more! In twelve-plus years of *WWHL*, I was most nervous when she was on. I wanted the show to be perfect and to be at my best for her. My respect for what she did on *The Oprah Winfrey Show* knows no bounds. I would tape it on VHS every day in high school, college, and afterwards. (By the way, to this day, that episode of *WWHL* remains one of our best.)

◊ *The Oprah Winfrey Show* premiered on September 8, 1986. Television was never the same!

SEPTEMBER 9

"I don't think of dying.
I think of being here now."

—Valerie Harper

Valerie Harper said this months after being diagnosed with brain cancer. I always loved her character Rhoda, and I found out years later that the actress herself had all the strength and character of a thousand Rhodas. So be a Rhoda today, in honor of Valerie.

◊ *Rhoda* premiered on CBS on September 9, 1974.

SEPTEMBER

"I'll tell you what freedom is to me. No fear."
—Nina Simone

Whether through her music or activism, Nina Simone defined "fearless" her entire life. No one can be completely free if they're afraid of being who they truly are or afraid of whatever bigotry society brings. We have more work to do to make freedom a reality for everyone.

◊ Nina Simone performed what she considered to be her first civil rights song, "Mississippi Goddam," on *The Steve Allen Show* on September 10, 1964. The song was already banned in several southern states, so this performance on a national talk show was significant.

SEPTEMBER

"I'm so glad we had this time together."
—Carol Burnett

Is there a more pure, honest way to end a show than Burnett's? I think it'd also work as a farewell as you're leaving someone's house. You gotta be earnest though, or it won't work.

◊ *The Carol Burnett Show* premiered on CBS on September 11, 1967.

12

SEPTEMBER

"I can't stand what people do to each other. I think we're brilliant as a species. I think we are amazing. I think that God is incredible, that He just gave us everything. Everything in our face. Everything for us to use. And sometimes we're such shitheads. And it makes me crazy."

—Pat Benatar

Do not mess with Pat Benatar when she tells you not to behave like a shithead. Actually, don't mess with Pat Benatar, period. And here's a Pat Benatar interlude: My father was notoriously mellow, but he would get annoyed by the most random stuff. In high school, I'd blast the twelve-inch vinyl of "Love Is a Battlefield" until the needle hit the end of the record, when it'd automatically pick back up and go back to the beginning of the song. Did I lose you with my record-player talk? Anyway, the endless loop of "We were young! Heartache to heartache!" caused my dad to break one night. And I never forgot it! Back to Pat's point: Don't act like a shithead.

◇ "Love Is a Battlefield" was released on this day in 1983.

13

SEPTEMBER

"My heart is broken in the face
of the stupidity of my species."

—Joni Mitchell

No offense to the human race, but Joni's right again. Never underestimate the stupidity of our fellow man. It's a good thing to keep in mind as one navigates through life in order to: a) make us feel better about ourselves, and b) keep our expectations of others in check.

◊ Joni Mitchell first performed her song "Woodstock" at the Big Sur Folk Festival on this day in 1969.

14
SEPTEMBER

"Better to live one year as a tiger
than a hundred as a sheep."
—Madonna

This is the spirit of Madonna that I love. And I'm pretty sure she's actually a tiger! (Also, see previous page and revel in the glory that neither Madonna nor Joni suffer fools.)

◇ On September 14, 1984, Madonna performed "Like a Virgin" at the first-ever VMAs, launching her into superstardom.

SEPTEMBER

"I'm such a whore, I can't say no."

—Betty White

I'm not sure I'd equate Betty to a whore, but she did when asked why she works so much. I've always respected Betty White's hustle, and her ability to play whores!

◊ Betty White's first appearance as Sue Ann Nivens on *The Mary Tyler Moore* show aired on September 15, 1973, in an episode called "The Lars Affair."

SEPTEMBER

"I eat morons like you for breakfast. You're
gonna be crying before this is over."
—Judy Sheindlin

Judge Judy gets paid a shit-ton of money to deal with an entire solar system of idiots. Imagine how fun it would be to yell at morons all day, make them do the right thing, and get paid for it! (Add Judy to the list of Ladies I Love Who Don't Suffer Fools!)

◊ *Judge Judy* premiered on September 16, 1996.

SEPTEMBER

"Is that a wig you're wearing?"

—Princess Margaret

Don't ask a woman if she's wearing a wig, even if you're Princess Margaret and you're talking to Mary Wilson from the Supremes. It's just wrong.

◊ The Supremes' hit song "Baby Love" was released on this date in 1964.

SEPTEMBER

"Sorry to this man."

—Keke Palmer

This quote went viral when Keke showed grace as she couldn't identify who Dick Cheney was in a picture. If you don't know someone, apologize and be polite. (Also, I wish I didn't know who Dick Cheney is . . .)

◇ Keke Palmer's debut studio album, *So Uncool*, was released on September 18, 2007.

SEPTEMBER

"I never expect anything I do to turn out well."
—Mary Tyler Moore

Mary always seemed so ... chirpy for so many years that it's surprising that this is who she really was. And it's a lesson that we don't always know what's going on inside someone's house.

◊ *The Mary Tyler Moore Show* premiered on September 19, 1970.

20 SEPTEMBER

"Be bold. If you're going to make an error, make a doozy, and don't be afraid to hit the ball."

—Billie Jean King

I suck at tennis. I really just want to live the lifestyle. I want to go to the tennis club on Saturday and stay in my whites and have lunch, then cocktails, all afternoon. Then I'd take Farrah home and make love to her before a sunset ocean walk. Anyway ...

◊ The famous "Battle of the Sexes" tennis match took place on this day in 1973. Billie Jean King defeated Bobby Riggs in three straight sets.

21 SEPTEMBER

"The people who present themselves as normal
and nice and good are often the scariest
monsters in the world."

—Catherine O'Hara

I can't stand a moralistic hypocrite and as a gay man have often found that the folks preaching values are the ones with a garage full of nasty secrets. Side note: No one plays scary monsters better than Catherine O'Hara!

◇ Catherine O'Hara was in the original cast of *Second City Television*, which premiered in Canada on September 21, 1976.

SEPTEMBER

"You can't pursue something and be committed to it if you're apologizing for it at every party."

—Lisa Kudrow

To further that thought, you can't half-ass something and expect to be successful doing it. You have to commit to whatever you want to do, the same way Lisa Kudrow committed to "Smelly Cat"! If you want to be a clown, then you better show up to that family reunion wearing a red nose and a wig!

◊ *Friends* premiered on September 22, 1994.

23 SEPTEMBER

"Do you remember what happened to Uncle Philip? He had a huge job with the government, and he started smoking grass, and he ended up working at Blockbuster video."

—Patricia Altschul

Don't be like Uncle Philip, ladies and gentlemen. We all need to remember him the next time we smoke a joint. Do it in moderation and don't freak out. You'll wind up at Blockbuster.

◊ The original Blockbuster company closed operations on September 23, 2010.

24

SEPTEMBER

"I never go outside unless I look like Joan Crawford the movie star. If you want to see the girl next door, go next door."

—Joan Crawford

I love to picture Joan Crawford snarling this line with great strength and authority. She said this in 1937, but she lived by the mantra till she died in 1977. Joan Crawford was a fierce bitch.

◊ Joan Crawford won an Academy Award for Best Actress for the film *Mildred Pierce*, which came out on this day in 1945.

25
SEPTEMBER

"If someone has the talent, they have the RIGHT
to be temperamental."

—Patti LuPone

I don't agree with this necessarily, but I love that Patti LuPone has not had a single fuck to give for many, many years. I will say that one does tend to forgive talented assholes more than we forgive just plain assholes.

◊ *Evita* premiered on Broadway on September 25, 1979, with Patti LuPone in the starring role.

SEPTEMBER 26

"I still love big jewelry."

—Jennifer Lopez

She's still Jenny from the block. She used to have a little; now she has a lot. And she still loves big jewelry. Never lose what you love.

◊ Lopez's signature hit song, "Jenny from the Block," was released on September 26, 2002.

SEPTEMBER 27

"Homophobia is like racism and anti-Semitism and other forms of bigotry in that it seeks to dehumanize a large group of people, to deny their humanity, their dignity and personhood. This sets the stage for further repression and violence that spread all too easily to victimize the next minority group."

—Coretta Scott King

Mrs. King said these inspiring words in 1998, and when I saw the quote, I dug into her history and found decades of support for the LGBTQ community from MLK's late wife. She supported gay and lesbian leaders in civil rights marches, used the King Center to educate people about HIV/AIDS, and strongly supported legislation to ban discrimination based on sexual orientation. She also spoke out against "Don't Ask, Don't Tell" in the '90s and a constitutional amendment banning same-sex marriage in the 2000s. I became more enamored with her the more I read.

◊ Coretta Scott King was the featured speaker at the September 27, 1986, New York Gala of the Human Rights Campaign Fund.

28
SEPTEMBER

"Own it, baby!"

—Lisa Rinna

Lisa Rinna originally shouted this at Kim Richards, but it became her mantra for years to come, and it's worthwhile. Own your weaknesses and turn them into strengths, the way Lisa wore doing Depends commercials as a badge in which she made major money!

◊ Lisa Rinna's final episode of *Days of Our Lives* as Billie Reed aired on September 28, 1995.

SEPTEMBER

"Girls, if a boy says something that isn't funny,
you don't have to laugh."

—Amy Poehler

This is very good advice for anyone in a position of having to laugh at a stupid joke. It's good for men to know when they're actually not funny.

◇ Amy Poehler's first episode as a cast member of *Saturday Night Live* aired on September 29, 2001.

30

SEPTEMBER

"It's so much easier to know who you are when there aren't a thousand people telling you who they think you are."

—Miley Cyrus

I'm confident that a thousand people didn't tell Miley they think she's a girl who sticks her tongue out on red carpets. In fact, the inspiration behind Miley's infamous "tongue slide" speaks to defying others' impressions of you. It began out of her insecurity about what to do while posing for pics. The photographers were telling her to blow a kiss, and she knew that wasn't her, so she stuck her tongue out, which became synonymous with Miley for years. Don't you love an origin story with a heart?

◊ Miley Cyrus's fourth album, *Bangerz,* which reinvented her entire image, was released on this day in 2013.

"Fashion changes, but style endures."

—Coco Chanel

Think about this the next time you consider spending a fortune on a wildly overpriced Gucci sweater with a lion on it. Is anyone going to be happy to see it in a year? Does it have legs, sweetie? The answer is usually no.

◊ It's National Consignment Day! (And I'm not sure Coco Chanel would be on board.)

OCTOBER

"I think that it is always worth it to stand by some basic principles, so if I've lost some roles because some distributor didn't like my politics, that's par for the course, as they used to say."

—Vanessa Redgrave

Vanessa Redgrave is a badass woman who has stood up for what she believed in, in the face of enormous personal and financial backlash, for her entire life. She's also an incredible actress and great fun shooting the curd by a fire with a margarita.

◊ Vanessa Redgrave's film *Julia* was released on October 2, 1977. She received an Academy Award for Best Supporting Actress for this role and made a controversial acceptance speech.

3

OCTOBER

"Let's put it this way: The older you get,
the easier it is to date younger men.
There are more of them."

—Connie Britton

And it's amazing how many of them like older women (and men)! So change your settings on your Tinder to an age you otherwise might not have considered, and let me know what happens!

◊ *Friday Night Lights* premiered on NBC on October 3, 2006.

OCTOBER

"Only God can judge me, and he seems
quite impressed."
—Phaedra Parks

Loving oneself seems to be a prerequisite to becoming a Real House-wife, and I love seeing the vanity of a Housewife in full bloom! We should all take a piece of confidence from these women and carry our heads a little higher. If they can, can't we?

◊ Phaedra Parks's first episode of *The Real Housewives of Atlanta* was the third-season premiere, which aired on October 4, 2010. This quote was her tagline for season 8.

OCTOBER

"As long as you dwell on the bad, it's taking the life away from you that you need to be living."

—Loretta Lynn

This is a lady who saw her share of hard times and hard livin', so listen to her speak. Side note: I got to sing "Louisiana Woman, Mississippi Man" with Loretta when she was on my show, and it remains a peak experience.

◇ Loretta Lynn's signature song, "Coal Miner's Daughter," was released on October 5, 1970.

OCTOBER

"See my men have stayed the same age . . .
I used to marry men 20 years old and they've
stayed the same age."

—Elizabeth Taylor

Yet another thing Liz and I have in common!

◊ Taylor's eighth, and final, wedding, to construction worker Larry Fortensky, took place on October 6, 1991.

OCTOBER

"Some people would find it strange that I decorate my office with pictures of myself, and what I have to say to you is 'eat shit and die.'"
—Kim Zolciak-Biermann

A real Real Housewife has absolutely no shame regarding pursuits that might be considered by others to be deeply rooted in narcissism. And I celebrate that!

◊ *The Real Housewives of Atlanta* premiered on Bravo on this day in 2008.

OCTOBER 8

"The three words every woman really longs
to hear: I'll clean up."
—Molly Shannon

Clean up after your women, men!!!!!! It gets them off! And if it doesn't, do that next!

◊ Molly Shannon's film *Superstar* was released on October 8, 1999.

OCTOBER

"Sometimes if I'm stuck on something, I'll have a drink, and it'll get me inspired and ready to keep going. But the trick to that, again, is that you have to drink responsibly! I've learned how to use it sometimes to help my creative process."

—Issa Rae

Though I drink on TV all the time and early in the run of *WWHL* would get shitcanned on air occasionally, it's smoking pot that gets my creative juices flowing, to say, write a book. If I get high before a massage, I often have to grab a pen after to make a list of brilliant ideas I had on the table. And five out of six of them hold up in the light of the next day! Be like me and Issa Rae: Find your vice!

◊ Issa Rae's series, *Insecure*, premiered on HBO on October 9, 2016.

"So I was in my chemistry lesson, in school, and just studying about atoms and those things. And suddenly my teacher came in, and she surprised me and said, 'You have won the Nobel Peace Prize,' and I said, 'Okay . . .'"

—Malala Yousafzai

I love this entire scenario, and it makes me wonder how on earth do you go back to your chemistry class after finding out you won the Nobel Prize?! If it was me, I'd have gone on whatever a high school bender looks like. Given what I know about Malala, she probably went right back to class, which is why she has a Nobel Prize and I don't. I did meet Malala at *Glamour*'s Women of the Year Awards, but she was too deep in conversation with Lady Gaga for me to find out what she did after she found out about the award!

◊ Malala Yousafzai was announced as a co-recipient of the 2014 Nobel Peace Prize on October 10, 2014.

OCTOBER 11

"I probably would have hated your wife
anyway."
—Evelyn Cohen

Through tears, my mom was able to slay me with this truth bomb
minutes after I'd come out of the closet to her. And I'm pretty sure she
would've hated my (poor) wife. So we all dodged some bullets.

◊ Happy National Coming Out Day!

12
OCTOBER

"We also have to focus on ourselves, because at the end of the day we're human, too. So we have to protect our mind and our body, rather than just go out there and do what the world wants us to do."
—Simone Biles

When Biles withdrew from the Tokyo Olympics to focus on her mental health, she faced a torrent of opinions from a Greek chorus who couldn't know what it's like to hurl backward ten feet in the air in front of the world. The judges may not award points for self-care and preservation, but the G.O.A.T.'s quick dismount got another perfect score from me.

◇ Check in with your mental health today, and every day!

13
OCTOBER

"You can have it all, but you can't do it all."
—Michelle Pfeiffer

You can be widely successful and have a happy, big family, but in the end we all have to make choices. You're only human. You literally cannot do every job or project you want to do and be there at every important moment for the people around you. That being said, Michelle Pfeiffer seems perfect, so she just may be able to.

◊ *The Fabulous Baker Boys* was released on this day in 1989.

"You're scared that Kim won't be able to use her
big fat ass to get you 10 percent."
—Khloe Kardashian

This little aside, said by Khloe to her mom, Kris, on an episode of
KUWTK is a perfect illustration of my theory that Khloe is the superior Kardashian, and for me it all comes back to her razor-sharp wit and ability to dismantle any situation in the blink of an eye. She gives her family tireless crap, says what everyone's thinking, and still comes out on top.

◊ *Keeping Up with the Kardashians* premiered on E! on October 14, 2007.

OCTOBER

"I don't know anything about luck. I've never
banked on it, and I'm afraid of people who do.
Luck to me is something else: hard work and
realizing what is opportunity and what isn't."

—Lucille Ball

W hen I was a kid, every time I went to our public library, I'd check
out the same book about the history of *I Love Lucy*. I'd get lost in the
behind-the-scenes stories about one of my favorite shows. I probably
read it twenty-five times, and every time I'd come home with it, my
mom would pitch a fit. "Again with the Lucy book!?!? Are there
any other books?" She thought I was either going to grow up to be an
idiot or work in TV. I did both!

◊ *I Love Lucy* premiered on CBS on this day in 1951.

16

OCTOBER

"A good trick is to fill your medicine cabinet with marbles. Nothing announces a nosey guest better than an avalanche of marbles hitting a porcelain sink. Plus you'll know which guest is a junkie whore or gutter hype, and you'll know what else to hide. Count your stash or remove the labels from your prescription bottles."

—Amy Sedaris

Amy has tips for days!

◊ Amy Sedaris's book *I Like You: Hospitality Under the Influence* was published on October 16, 2006.

17

OCTOBER

"It was hard for me to really like myself. I had to
really learn how to love myself, and I'm at that
point now to really accept me for who I am.
That was very difficult for me in my twenties,
in my thirties."

—Janet Jackson

Yet another thing that Janet—Miss Jackson, if you're nasty—and I
have in common. I had a ball in my twenties and thirties—hell, I still
am—but I think I really settled into myself in my forties, and by fifty
I knew exactly who I was. You on my clock, too?

◊ Janet Jackson's hit song "Control" was released on October 17, 1986.

18 OCTOBER

"I always think, after the second glass of wine, you should be putting something in your stomach."

—Padma Lakshmi

This isn't revolutionary, but it's an opportunity for me to say that Padma is so fun to drink anything with, and she's great at helping pad your stomach so you can drink more!

◊ Padma Lakshmi's first episode as host of *Top Chef* aired on this day in 2006.

OCTOBER

"I think that the longer I look good,
the better gay men feel."

—Cher

I think she's right, by the way. I think seeing Cher looking great releases endorphins in gay guys. From the minute Cher showed up in my life singing down a ramp on the *Cher* show (who needed Sonny?), I couldn't take my eyes off her hair, her clothes, her odd tic with her tongue ... Adoring women is a big part of my life, and I'd recommend that all women find themselves one great gay friend because they will always prop you up and celebrate you. That's one of the things we're here to do: Celebrate women.

◇ Cher's song "Believe" was released on October 19, 1998, and quickly became one of the biggest-selling singles of all time. The song is known for its use of Auto-Tune, also called the "Cher effect."

OCTOBER

"The only person who can hack me is me!
I ain't shy. If you want to see Leslie Jones
naked, just ask."

—Leslie Jones

Context: After she was hacked and her nudes leaked, she gave a master class in "owning it" (see: Lisa Rinna) on "Weekend Update."

◊ Leslie Jones was promoted to the *Saturday Night Live* cast as a featured player on October 20, 2014.

OCTOBER

"Everyone probably thinks that I'm a raving nymphomaniac, that I have an insatiable sexual appetite, when the truth is I'd rather read a book."
—Madonna

This is helpful for all of us who suffer from FOMO, or jealousy. We may THINK Madonna is doing tantric yoga with a twenty-three-year-old Brazilian backup dancer while we're home watching the *Housewives*, but she's probably home, too, albeit reading about Frida Kahlo. Now, I might even argue that watching the *Housewives* is more fun than reading about Frida Kahlo at home, and this is my way of telling you that you're having more fun than Madonna.

◊ Madonna's book *Sex* was published on October 21, 1992.

"I think husbands and wives should live in separate houses. If there's enough money, the children should live in a third."
—Cloris Leachman

Wouldn't that be divine? We all need our personal space. For starters: No one would have to deal with the reality of everyone's bathroom needs. It's fun to think about, but we'd miss our kids.

◊ Cloris Leachman's film *The Last Picture Show* was theatrically released on this day in 1971. She won an Academy Award for Best Supporting Actress for her role in the movie.

23 OCTOBER

"The cool thing about being famous is traveling.
I have always wanted to travel across seas,
like to Canada and stuff."

—Britney Spears

Oops, she did it again! She tricked you into thinking what she was saying was cotton candy flimflam while expressing a truism. Traveling IS a great perk of fame, and it's indeed the great perk of life itself. I consider traveling and real estate my two greatest indulgences. Traveling well and living in a home you love are two keys to happiness. Thanks for taking us on another metaphorical journey, Britney!

◇ Britney Spears's first single, "Baby One More Time," was released on October 23, 1998.

OCTOBER 24

"Out of Myself, Britney, and Christina—
didn't everyone think I was gonna be the
troublemaker? LOOK MA!!! No CUFFS!!!"
—P!nk

I, too, would've bet the farm that P!nk would've been the problematic one of these three. The exclamation point in her name seems like she's begging for trouble. She's not only a badass without a record; she can sing while performing aerial stunts!

◊ P!nk's fifth studio album, *Funhouse*, was released on October 24, 2008.

OCTOBER

"I'm probably the only person over forty who does not want to be twenty-two again."
—Monica Lewinsky

I love the way Monica has embraced her past with humor and intelligence. She turned something truly horrible into a learning experience. I've gotten to know her over the past decade, and she stops traffic anytime she's around. As famous as she is, she's incredibly down-to-earth and kind. She even knitted a gorgeous winter hat for Ben when he was born!

◊ On this day in 1881, Pablo Picasso was born!

26
OCTOBER

"I'm not looking for a man. Let's start there."
—Rihanna

This Rihanna clapback to a reporter who asked what she's looking for in a man IS IT!!!!!!!

◊ Rihanna's hit single "What's My Name?" was released on October 26, 2010.

OCTOBER

"I can dress in the toilet. Don't matter to me.
I came to sing for the people,
that's all I want to do."

—Gladys Knight

The lesson here is that the next time Diana Ross steals your dressing room while on tour, remember why you're there in the first place and get dressed in the can. I'm sure we can apply this to our own lives, but the thought of Diana stealing Gladys's dressing room is too delicious to pass up.

◊ Gladys Knight & the Pips had their first No. 1 hit on the *Billboard* Hot 100 when "Midnight Train to Georgia" reached the top spot on this day in 1973.

28
OCTOBER

"Stop singing my part now, baby."
—Mariah Carey

The year is 2008. Mariah Carey is promoting her newest album $E=MC^2$ on *GMA* with a performance of "Touch My Body." The performance gets off to a rocky start as the track plays and Mariah misses her cue to sing, but then about three minutes in, she sings this quote at a background singer and then proceeds to belt out her signature multi-octave voice. A true diva knows how to save a performance and put someone in their place without missing the beat.

◊ Mariah Carey's timeless Christmas classic, "All I Want for Christmas Is You," was released on October 28, 1994.

OCTOBER

"One of the greatest things my therapist said to
me . . . and it really blew my mind in
the greatest way, he just said,
'Look in the mirror less.'"

—Sarah Silverman

I'm thinking Sarah Silverman may be my new rabbi. Or her therapist
might be. That being said, do make sure you don't have lipstick in your
teeth or Naomi Campbell will cut you.

◊ Don't look in the mirror today! Try it!

OCTOBER

"I used to want to be tall, and then I thought, 'If I were tall, then people would say I was pretty and not cute.' And then I realized that there are worse things than being called cute. They could say I was a bitch, which would be terrible in my book. So I've decided that this height ain't so bad."

—Kristin Chenoweth

Here's another reason I love all four feet eleven inches of this pint-sized scene stealer: She's got enough of a sense of humor about herself to twice play a game on *WWHL* called "Fit It! or Quit It!" in which we predict whether she can fit into clothes made for toddlers. Not only did she fit into several of the items; she took home a sweater she loved! Side note: Watching Kristin Chenoweth try on toddler clothes is wildly entertaining!

◊ Kristin Chenoweth starred in the musical *Wicked*, which opened on Broadway on October 30, 2003. (I was there!)

31
OCTOBER

"You should never say bad things about the dead, you should only say good . . . Joan Crawford is dead. Good."

—Bette Davis

I'm someone who loves to challenge the line of good taste and decorum, and this quote does just that. It gets a laugh from me because of how much these two legends hated each other. Each was nasty in her own way, but keeping the feud going even after one is six feet under is a level of pettiness that must be acknowledged.

◊ Happy Halloween! The film *What Ever Happened to Baby Jane?* starring Bette Davis and Joan Crawford, was released in the United States on this day in 1962.

"The only time a woman really succeeds in changing a man is when he is a baby."
—Natalie Wood

I wonder what the human race could have accomplished with all the time wasted on trying to change men.

◊ Natalie Wood's film *Gypsy* was released on November 1, 1962.

2 NOVEMBER

"But this is not the greatest moment of my life because on Friday, I had a really great baked potato at Nibblers on Wilshire."

—Lily Tomlin

This nugget came from Lily Tomlin as she accepted an Emmy in 1974 for Outstanding Comedy-Variety, Variety or Music Special for her show *Lily*. Nibblers Baked Potato > Emmy = a woman with perspective!

◇ In November 1975, Tomlin became the sixth-ever person to host *SNL*, and the second woman to do so after another woman I love, Candice Bergen.

3
NOVEMBER

"To be a revolutionary you have to be a human being. You have to care about people who have no power."

—Jane Fonda

Jane Fonda is full of humanity, passion, and drive. Her upright presence fills each room she enters, and she is completely present in herself as well. I want to be like Jane Fonda when I grow up.

◊ Jane Fonda posed for her famous mug shot on November 3, 1970, for trumped-up charges of drug smuggling on orders from the Nixon White House.

4
NOVEMBER

"I can't pretend."

—Chaka Khan

This is Chaka Khan on *WWHL* talking about the miserable time she had at Oprah's Legends Ball, an event I would've given my left arm to attend! This was Oprah's event celebrating black women of excellence, a party with a better guest list than any Oscar party or Met Gala I'd ever seen. Chaka said she went in very happy and excited to be there, but by the end was tired and annoyed. Indeed the group picture shows her looking completely over it, even as she stood next to Michelle Obama! She's every woman, indeed!

◊ Chaka Khan's song "Ain't Nobody" was released on November 4, 1983.

NOVEMBER 5

"Service is the rent that you pay for room on this earth."
—Shirley Chisholm

This is a wonderful philosophy that should be imparted to all of us as we go through our lives.

◇ On November 5, 1968, Shirley Chisholm became the first Black woman elected to the United States Congress, representing New York's Twelfth Congressional District.

NOVEMBER

"Why would you trust a girl that has tits bigger than her head?"

—Tamra Judge

With the exception of Dolly Parton, I'm gonna take this one to the bank. Fun fact: Pretty much every woman who started on the *Real Housewives* with massive fake boobs wound up having them reduced. There's a lesson in there. I just don't know it yet.

◊ Tamra Judge's first episode of *The Real Housewives of Orange County* was the season 3 premiere, which aired on November 6, 2007.

NOVEMBER

"Being a perfectionist is not an evil thing."
—Martha Stewart

How many strong women have had to repeat this sentiment—Streisand, Ross, Franklin—and each one is a genius, so they prove their point well.

◊ *Martha & Snoop's Potluck Dinner Party* premiered on VH1 on November 7, 2016.

8

NOVEMBER

"Realize that looking the other way and hoping that everything will work out later is a foolish idea."

—Claire McCaskill

Claire said this in her final speech on the Senate floor. Claire is forever a pragmatist, and I adored her as my senator from Missouri. She's great on MSNBC with a cake behind her, too. But I prefer her in DC.

◊ Claire McCaskill was elected to the United States Senate on November 8, 2006.

NOVEMBER

"I dyed my hair this crazy red to bid for
attention. It has become a trademark and I've
got to keep it this way."

—Lucille Ball

If you have a gimmick, stick with it. I will say in the last years of Lucy's life when she would show up at award shows with fire-engine red hair, I used to wonder whether she should give it up, but I appreciate her consistency.

◊ Lucille Ball became the first female head of a major television studio, Desilu Productions, on this day in 1962.

NOVEMBER 10

"The only power you have is the word no."
—Frances McDormand

People underestimate how powerful that word is and forget that in most cases, no explanation is needed. It's perfectly acceptable to decline an invitation or request by just saying no. And it feels great!

◊ Frances McDormand's film *Three Billboards Outside Ebbing, Missouri* was released in the United States on November 10, 2017.

11
NOVEMBER

"Thank you. I'm disengaging. I'm not engaging."
—Meredith Marks

Disengaging when things get too hot in the proverbial kitchen isn't necessarily what we want to see from our Housewives, but for those of us who aren't on the *Real Housewives* (and that's 99.999999 percent of the people reading this book), I think it's an attitude that could serve us in daily life when people around us are behaving like assholes!

◊ Meredith Marks appears in *The Real Housewives of Salt Lake City*, which premiered on Bravo on this day in 2020.

NOVEMBER

"I don't want to spend my life in my 40s feeling
bad about being in my 40s, and then all
of a sudden I'm 50, and I will have missed
a whole decade!"

—Laura Linney

First of all, let's take a moment to acknowledge the wonder of Laura Linney looking the same in every decade of her life. She and I are both on the "have a kid at fifty train," and certainly sharing this philosophy about aging led us both to be comfortable jumping out of the proverbial plane when we were more settled in our lives. Say your age with strength in your voice, no matter where you are in life.

◊ Laura Linney's film *Kinsey* was released theatrically on November 12, 2004.

NOVEMBER 13

"Don't keep a man guessing too long—he's sure to find the answer somewhere else."

—Mae West

Mae had it absolutely right, and she said this in 1967, well before Grindr and Tinder and every available means to instant gratification. Life and technology may change, but the notion that men are dogs is timeless.

◊ Mae West's film *Go West, Young Man* was released in the United States on November 13, 1936.

NOVEMBER 14

"Some people do drugs and go out every weekend. I built a water park."

—Celine Dion

Sometimes when you're the greatest singer in the world, you come off wacky, but it doesn't matter because you're the greatest singer in the world!

◇ Celine Dion's album *Let's Talk About Love* was released on November 14, 1997, and went on to become one of the best-selling albums in history, selling more than 31 million copies worldwide.

15 NOVEMBER

"I deserve this. Thank you."

—Shirley MacLaine

Sounds like she did deserve her Academy Award after her tumultuous relationship with Debra Winger in *Terms of Endearment*. Did Winger fart on Shirley? I don't know, but I deserved an Emmy after trying to question Winger about it on *WWHL* years later!

◇ Shirley MacLaine's film *Steel Magnolias* was released on November 15, 1989.

"I'm way too annoying because I get on red carpets and I'm really hyper. Most likely because I've been drinking, and I can't not photobomb somebody if it's a good opportunity . . . But it's something I always tell myself: 'You need to calm the f—k down. You don't want to constantly be a GIF.'"

—Jennifer Lawrence

I am incredibly hyperactive in front of cameras, and I tend to over-modulate (scream) on talk shows. I plan to keep this quote in my back pocket as a personal warning to try to calm the hell down.

◊ Make a plan to do something fun today!

NOVEMBER

"See you at the next thing!"

—Gayle King

I love running into Gayle—and we've run into each other all over the place—because I know I'm somewhere fun if she shows up. And this comment is what she always leaves me with. I love it because it signifies a continuation of life . . . the party is going on somewhere else, and we'll see each other then.

◇ Gayle King's final episode as host of OWN's *The Gayle King Show* aired on November 17, 2011, due to her moving on to co-anchor *CBS This Morning*.

NOVEMBER

"I arrived in Hollywood without having my nose fixed, my teeth capped, or my name changed. That is very gratifying to me."

—Barbra Streisand

Can you imagine the horror of Streisand with the same nose as everyone on *The Real Housewives of Beverly Hills*? No offense to my Wives, but would her voice still sound the same if she'd gone under Dr. Klein's knife? Would her spirit be intact? I love that she forever blazed her own trail. (I still mispronounce her name all the time but that's a me problem.)

◊ With the release of *Yentl* on November 18, 1983, Barbra Streisand became the first woman to write, produce, direct, and star in a major studio film.

NOVEMBER

19

"I've read memoirs, some of them are good . . .
a lot of folks just need to have a diary."

—Stacey Abrams

And I've heard a lot of podcasts; some of them are good . . . a lot of
folks just need to call their friends.

◊ President Biden was officially declared the winner in Georgia after a recount in the
2020 election on November 19, 2020. He won the state in large part due to the work of
Stacey Abrams and other Black activists.

NOVEMBER

"Whatever your reason for holding on to resentments, I know this for sure: There is none worth the price you pay in lost time."

—Oprah Winfrey

Another three-pointer from Lady O. Give this woman a car.

◊ Oprah Winfrey was awarded the Presidential Medal of Freedom on this day in 2013.

21
NOVEMBER

"People don't take interest in their appearance in going to the theater. They come in blue jeans cut up to here . . . the girls look like they're ready for a strip act or something."

—Ethel Merman

If you're in showbiz in New York, one of your favorite pastimes is to complain about how schlumpy people look when they go to a Broadway show. It's not a movie. It's not Vegas. *It's Broadway!* I loved discovering that none other than Ethel Merman complained about this very thing back in 1977!

◊ Ethel Merman's musical *Anything Goes* opened on Broadway on November 21, 1934.

22 NOVEMBER

"Being offended is a natural consequence of leaving one's home."

—Fran Lebowitz

I wish I knew she felt this way before she shared her offense at the *Housewives* to me at a fashion show once; I'd have realized not to take it personally!

◊ *Public Speaking*, a documentary about Fran Lebowitz directed by Martin Scorsese, was released in the United States on this day in 2010.

NOVEMBER

"The good news is hopeful doesn't mean dumb.
The bad news is cynical doesn't mean smart."

—Sarah Silverman

Let me put this another way: Being cynical is often fun and might seem to give you the higher ground, but it often just makes you look like an asshole.

◊ The HBO stand-up special *Sarah Silverman: We Are Miracles* premiered on November 23, 2013.

NOVEMBER 24

"If I smell milk . . . I can't be bothered."
—Chaka Khan

This was Chaka Khan telling Wendy Williams about her disdain for dating men who are too young. I agree that relationships with much younger fellas won't go the mile, but I would argue that some dalliances are fun enough that they'll keep you young. (Also, I hate milk.)

◊ Chaka Khan was the first R&B artist to have a crossover hit featuring a rapper with "I Feel for You," which peaked at No. 3 on the *Billboard* Hot 100 on this day in 1984.

25
NOVEMBER

"It wasn't a walk of shame. It was a lap of victory at my age."

—Sonja Morgan

I love women who own their sexuality, and I always view *The Real Housewives of New York* as role models in that regard. (Go with me here.) They're sexually free, have sex on their own terms, and they look and feel great about it. Isn't that how we all should be?

26
NOVEMBER

"On the way home, I go, 'So, how long have you been dating your mother?' and that was the end of the relationship."

—Rosie Perez

Rosie Perez said this to a boyfriend after she witnessed his mother waiting on him hand and foot. There's never a winner in a competition against someone's mom.

◊ Rosie Perez's series *The Flight Attendant* premiered on HBO Max on November 26, 2020.

27
NOVEMBER

"You can have anything you want in life if you dress for it."

—Edith Head

Edith Head was the most famous costume designer in Hollywood for decades, and this prescription for style was right on. I always kick it up a notch when I'm getting dressed for a big day, and looking good makes me better from posture to performance.

◊ Edith Head's first big achievement in costume design was Dorothy Lamour's trademark sarong in the film *The Jungle Princess*, which was released on this day in 1936.

NOVEMBER 28

"I designed my whole image. That was all me. I just bought some regular clothes, threw a medallion around my neck, and that was it. The next thing I know, that's the look."

—Queen Latifah

I always admire someone who went with their gut and started a movement—fashion or otherwise.

◊ Queen Latifah's debut studio album, *All Hail the Queen*, was released on November 28, 1989.

29

NOVEMBER

"I believe there should be no more drama, but it's everywhere you go. It's just about how you get out. You've gotta bob and weave because it's everywhere. How do I keep the drama low? It's about using your head."

—Mary J. Blige

I believe Mary J. Blige should run for office using "No More Drama" as her platform. It's a universally appealing idea! We all should embrace it! (Except everyone on Bravo.)

◊ Mary J. Blige's second, and breakthrough, studio album, *My Life*, was released on November 29, 1994.

NOVEMBER

"The most important thing for having a party is that the hostess is having fun."

—Ina Garten

Ina, why are you so perfect? I couldn't agree more about this one. I go to a lot of parties and am often amazed by people's inability to throw them. This sounds very cocky, but some of the best parties I've been to have been my own—and that takes confidence in yourself, your guest list, lighting, music, and what you serve. I have a holiday party every year that's the embodiment of a wild house party. I try to mix up the guest list and ensure that it has the legs to go as late as possible. If you can't have fun at your party, will your guests?

◊ Ina Garten's *Barefoot Contessa* premiered November 30, 2002, on Food Network.

1
DECEMBER

"I did not get on the bus to get arrested. I got on the bus to go home."
—Rosa Parks

One spark can start a revolution, and sometimes all it takes is standing up for what you believe in.

◊ Rosa Parks was arrested in Montgomery, Alabama, on this day in 1955, after she refused to give up her bus seat.

DECEMBER

"If you have to talk to more than three people
about the same problem, you don't want help,
you want attention."
—Naomi Campbell

Real Housewives doing this on camera are exempt from this sentiment, because it's in their DNA, but all others need to consider this
advice. Also, one might ask themselves if their problem is that interesting to be bugging all their friends about it?

◇ Naomi Campbell was the first Black woman to appear on the cover of British *Vogue*,
in the December 1987 issue.

DECEMBER 3

"I have been a waitress, and I was a damn fine
waitress, too, let me tell you."
—Jessica Lange

Waiting tables is a great job I'd recommend to anyone. I, too, was a fantastic server. I was a great multitasker, loved interacting with people, and nothing beat the accomplishment I felt going home with pockets stuffed with hard-earned cash.

◊ Jessica Lange's film *Frances* was released on December 3, 1982.

DECEMBER

"When haters go after your looks and differences, it means they have nowhere left to go. And then you know you're winning!"
—Greta Thunberg

◇

That a teenaged Thunberg had the maturity to put this into perspective as the president of the United States was attacking her for her—gasp—environmental activism tells you all you need to know about this young woman. Keep winning, Greta!

◊ Greta Thunberg addressed the 2018 United Nations Climate Change Conference on this day in 2018.

DECEMBER 5

"Where're my background singers?"
—Patti LaBelle

Miss Patti uttered, repeated, and demanded those words as she sang at the 1996 National Christmas Tree Lighting in a clip that's gone viral almost every Christmas since. She was lost, not only without her background singers, but the teleprompter didn't have the words to her song "This Christmas." But she carried on, and of course prevailed. And we should all repeat this as a mantra that allows us to move through life without our background singers, whoever they might metaphorically be. We can do this alone! We got this! Just like Patti!

◊ Patti LaBelle asked this question while performing "This Christmas" at the National Christmas Tree Lighting Ceremony on this day in 1996.

DECEMBER

"Fifty is the new thirty. Seventy is the new fifty.
There are no rules that say you have to dress a
certain way, or be a certain way. We are living
in exciting times for women."

—Tina Turner

Isn't it wonderfully empowering how our perception of age keeps moving as we cross each of life's goalposts? Further, to see someone like Tina Turner cross those lines before us makes us lean into what's ahead. If I run for office, I'll suggest chain-link miniskirts as the uniforms in old folks homes coast-to-coast!

° Tina Turner's eighth concert tour, the Twenty Four Seven Tour, ended its 108-show run on December 6, 2000. She was sixty!

DECEMBER

"If you can't imagine it, you can't have it."

—Toni Morrison

Was Toni the inspiration for Aerosmith's "Dream On"?! Her imagination was so large it produced some of the most powerful, important, and enduring works in all of literature. She imagined not only an incredible life for herself but inspires all of us to do so.

◊ Toni Morrison accepted the Nobel Prize in Literature on December 7, 1993. She was the first African American woman to win the award.

DECEMBER 8

"I want to feel my life while I'm in it."

—Meryl Streep

I want to feel Meryl Streep's life, too! Just do what Meryl says: Feel your life—feel it all, baby!

◊ Meryl Streep won an Oscar for Best Actress for *Sophie's Choice*, which was released on December 8, 1982.

DECEMBER 9

"People come for me all the time;
they just don't find me."
—Karen Huger

Haters are going to hate, but nothing they can say affects me. I am
(and Karen Huger is) untouchable.

◇ La'Dame Fragrance by Karen Huger launched on HSN on December 9, 2019.

DECEMBER

"I'm not the girl who gets to make out with Ryan Gosling in a scene. I'm the housekeeper who comes in on Ryan Gosling, and then I do a spit take and then trip over his underwear and knock my head as I walk out on all fours. That's my part. So I think there's longevity . . . I really think, if you are funny, I don't think age has anything to do with it, honestly."

—Andrea Martin

There's power and endurance in being funny and having a sense of humor—whether it's in the entertainment world or in an office. A sense of humor about life, and our place in it, I've found is essential to survive and thrive. Also, google Andrea Martin performing "No Time at All" from *Pippin*. All I'm saying is Ryan Gosling would be lucky to make out with HER in a movie.

◇ Andrea Martin won a Tony for Best Featured Actress in a Musical for *My Favorite Year*, which opened on Broadway on December 10, 1992.

11
DECEMBER

"I don't like bite-size brownies and I don't like cocktail sausages."
—Phaedra Parks

Wait, what are you talking about, Phaedra? I'm just not getting the reference!? And I'm pretty sure we all agree with you.

◊ *Phine Body by Phaedra & Apollo Donkey Booty Volume 1* was released on this day in 2012.

DECEMBER

"Here is my biggest takeaway after 60 years on
the planet: There is great value in being fearless.
For too much of my life, I was too afraid,
too frightened by it all. That fear is one
of my biggest regrets."

—Diane Keaton

This blows my mind because my image of Diane Keaton, based on her outward appearance and vibe, is that of a fearless woman. Who can pull off a men's suit and be full of fear? Perhaps this explains how Diane is able to truly lose herself in her famous hysterical cries. No one knows how to wail and scream better in a romantic comedy than Diane.

◊ Diane Keaton's film *Something's Gotta Give* was released in the United States on December 12, 2003.

DECEMBER

"All the things I love is what my business is all
about."

—Martha Stewart

I hope everyone can find jobs that allow them to do things that they
love and maybe even, like Martha, build a multimillion-dollar empire.
I'm blessed that my work rarely seems like work because talking and
loving TV have been two things I've enjoyed my whole life!

◊ Martha Stewart's first cookbook, *Entertaining*, was published on December 13, 1982.

14
DECEMBER

"Titties on fleek all day every day."
—Cardi B

Cardi's love for her own breasts is nothing short of inspiring. Whatever you love about yourself, whether it be a body part or your personality, make sure it is always on fleek.

◊ Cardi B's first episode of *Love & Hip Hop: New York* aired on December 14, 2015.

15
DECEMBER

"When I first heard that the sun is ninety-three million miles away from Earth, I thought, There's nothing more to learn. What else is there? Nothing."

—Cloris Leachman

Way to put it in perspective, Cloris! I need to note that making out with Leachman on *WWHL* was one of my favorite moments on the show!

◊ Cloris Leachman's film *Young Frankenstein* came out on December 15, 1974.

16

DECEMBER

"I really think that to a lot of people hair is everything. Bad hair takes over everything, it really does. I think if somebody has bad hair it doesn't matter what else is happening."

—Goldie Hawn

Now I know why Goldie's classic hairdo has remained for all these years—it really can mess a person up when you get it wrong. Now excuse me while I do a deep dive trying to figure out when Goldie got it wrong enough to have this thought . . .

◊ The first major film that Goldie Hawn starred in (and won the Oscar for Best Supporting Actress for), *Cactus Flower*, came out on December 16, 1969.

DECEMBER 17

"As long as you know men are like children,
you know everything!"
—Coco Chanel

I always remind friends that men think with their penises, but Coco really broadened that thought and flattened the male species as she did it. But I don't disagree.

◊ Coco Chanel designed the costumes for the film *Tonight or Never*, which was released theatrically on this day in 1931.

18
DECEMBER

"Oh, how I regret not having worn a bikini for the entire year I was twenty-six. If anyone young is reading this, go, right this minute, put on a bikini, and don't take it off until you're thirty-four."

—Nora Ephron

I saw some bathing suit pictures of myself in my thirties the other day and marveled at my torso and sadly remembered how fat I thought I was! If you're under forty, go shirtless as much as you can. Do it for me.

◊ Nora Ephron directed, produced, and wrote the screenplay for *You've Got Mail*, which was released in the United States on December 18, 1998.

"I like being called butter face because it implies
I have a dope body."

—Chrissy Teigen

✧

Now THIS is a hot take, and a brilliant way to turn a negative into a positive. Long live Chrissy.

◊ Chrissy Teigen's first big break was as a briefcase model on the first season of *Deal or No Deal*, which premiered on December 19, 2005.

DECEMBER 20

"I've loved all my jobs, even when I worked at
Burger King."
—Jennifer Hudson

I would pay triple the price to have J.Hud serve me a whopper, and if
anyone from BK is reading this, I suggest hiring her to bring back the
"Have It Your Way" jingle ASAP! Regarding her thought, don't forget
where you came from!

◊ The film musical *Cats* was released on December 20, 2019. It was terrible.

DECEMBER 21

"I have my standards. They're low, but I have them."

—Bette Midler

Speaking of gay icons ... I love Bette. And I also love that she said this funny remark on *One on One with Katie Couric*. No shade, but does anyone but Katie have any memory of this show's existence? I loved the era of female news superstars who did important, news-making, agenda-setting interviews!

◊ Bette Midler's film *Beaches*, which featured the song "Wind Beneath My Wings," came out on December 21, 1988.

22

DECEMBER

"Sex appeal is 50 per cent what you've got—
and 50 per cent what people think you've got."

—Sophia Loren

This is rich coming from a woman drenched in purely physical sex appeal. She'd be sexy if she were a timid wallflower, but throw in her attitude, and she over-indexes. But her advice is well taken. I have become transfixed by some real hatchet faces who've captured my attention with their certain je ne sais quoi. It works!

◇ The film *Two Women* premiered in Milan on December 22, 1960. Sophia Loren won the Academy Award for Best Actress the following year, making her the first actor or actress to win an acting Oscar for a foreign language performance.

23
DECEMBER

"I want a man who's kind and understanding. Is that too much to ask of a millionaire?"
—Zsa Zsa Gabor

Zsa Zsa strikes again! She was, as they say, of her time, but she was a gloriously madcap, funny Hungarian who loved to flaunt her taste for caviar and diamonds. I respect any woman who is clear about her needs and intentions, especially one who can do it with humor.

◊ Zsa Zsa Gabor's film *Moulin Rouge* was released in the United States on December 23, 1952.

DECEMBER

"Grief is the price we pay for love."

—Queen Elizabeth II

The queen said this in response to 9/11—it's true and beautiful. Side note: I know *The Crown* is not entirely real, but it left me with a lot of respect for the queen and helped crystallize the monarchy's actual meaning as a steady hand for the nation.

⸰ Enjoy the Queen's annual Christmas address tomorrow!

25

DECEMBER

"Living is like tearing through a museum. Not until later do you really start absorbing what you saw, thinking about it, looking it up in a book, and remembering—because you can't take it all in at once."

—Audrey Hepburn

Taking things in is one of the most important things we can do as we live our lives. Everything goes too damn fast.

◊ Audrey Hepburn's film *My Fair Lady* was released in the United States on Christmas Day in 1964.

26 DECEMBER

"I'm not super, super religious. If this is okay to say, I'm more culturally Jewish."
—Abbi Jacobson

I say this all the time about my relationship with Judaism, and I'm grateful that it's something I identify with and have my whole life. It took me finding a LGBT synagogue (CBST in NYC) for me to really get "into" my religion as an adult, but I love the traditions and am excited to pass them on to my kids.

◇ Happy final day of Hanukkah! (Based on 2022 calendar.)

27

DECEMBER

"I'd kill all of them."

—Kathy Bates

This was Kathy Bates's response when I asked her on *WWHL* to shag, marry, kill Jack Nicholson, Woody Allen, James Caan. I just think it's brilliant. I love a ballsy broad with zero fs to give.

◊ Kathy Bates's film *Fried Green Tomatoes* was released on December 27, 1991.

DECEMBER

"Bevelation: Finding a 'happy medium' is
settling, and the only time settling is good is
when it concerns a facelift or ass implants; then
you want things to settle. Otherwise, it's not a
good thing."
—Bevy Smith

And on that note, don't judge people right after they've had a facelift.
The face needs time to, as Bevy says, settle. It's a real thing! Give that
face six months to a year to tell you where it's going.

◊ It's the end of the year: Take stock of yourself, inside and out!

DECEMBER

"People ask me how I stay happy and sane: I never google myself."

—Miley Cyrus

If I googled myself, I'd discover I'm a walleyed single TV host who (fill in with a name) is mad at because I said (fill in with stupid comment). Thus, take it from Miley. However, you have my permission to google anyone you're meeting for a drink.

◊ "See You Again," the lead single from the album *Meet Miley Cyrus* was released on this day in 2007.

DECEMBER

"You're playing marbles on the Lord's coattail."

—Evelyn Cohen

My mom got this one from her dad, but she's used it as a warning to me throughout my life to mean that I'm playing with fire, and most likely testing her patience and authority. Since I loved to push things as far as I could, my response often included winking at her, which half the time resulted in her laughing and stopping screaming at me. (See also: "Get a hold of yourself!")

◊ I like starting and ending a year with mildly threatening quotes from my mother!

31
DECEMBER

"Be the woman you want to be."
—Diane von Furstenberg

DVF has been saying this for years, and I often tell her that I'm the woman I want to be.

◊ Happy birthday, DVF!

ACKNOWLEDGMENTS

Thank you to my incredible, intrepid researcher Lukas Thimm, who shares my passion for strong women, and whose encyclopedic knowledge of pop culture and politics fueled the creation of this book!

Thanks to Hoda Kotb for giving me the idea for this book.

Also thanks to my partners at Holt: Amy Einhorn, James Melia, Maggie Richards, and Pat Eisemann.

Andy Cohen is the author of three *New York Times* bestselling books, beginning with *Most Talkative*. He is the host and executive producer of *Watch What Happens Live*, Bravo's late-night, interactive talk show. He also serves as executive producer of the *Real Housewives* franchise and hosts the network's highly rated reunion specials. He's won an Emmy and two Peabody Awards for his work, and he lives in New York City.